MW01011590

Praise for *Up from Nothing*

"John takes us back to an idea of America where all can win. Instead of getting mired down by envy, greed, hate, and despair, John challenges us to rise up with positive thinking, self-confidence, aspiration, and hope—and to do it together."
—**Brad Hanson, President and Chief Executive Officer, Meta Financial Group and Metabank**

"John Hope Bryant's personal journey and professional accomplishments are an inspiration for me and many others. And the lessons that can be drawn from his experience have significant implications for all of us as leaders. In particular, his focus on the importance of mindset—the power of believing in oneself and having faith in those around you—is a critical insight for all of us. He helps us remember to see the best in ourselves and others and to convey that confidence to them. When we do this, we can unlock an enormous amount of potential in people and collectively achieve goals that no one ever thought possible."
—**Timothy Welsh, Vice Chair, Consumer and Business Banking, U.S. Bancorp**

"In *Up from Nothing*, John Hope Bryant has captured the essence of America's next societal challenge—to shed our fascination with division and instead focus on actions that will cement our standing as the greatest nation in the world. This book celebrates and elevates the ideas at the core of the American Dream—that success means choosing your own terms, that the future is more important than the past, and that self-worth is the most valuable asset of all."
—**Dallas Tanne, cofounder, President, and CEO, Invitation Homes**

"Reading this book was both informative and transformative. Whether we come from the hollers of Appalachia or the inner cities of LA, all of us battle the same obstacles and search for the same answers. The five foundational pillars Bryant identifies to ensure a level playing field of opportunity for all are brought to life through his biographical journey, which teaches us through applied experience while inspiring us with possibility and the desire to implement change immediately. Simply amazing!"
—**Brad D. Smith, Executive Chairman, Intuit**

"Sometimes it can be hard to really understand the plight of others when your personal experiences have been vastly different. It is difficult to know what is unseen. John Hope Bryant has lived many different lives and is successful in a diverse number of social and economic circles, which he shares in *Up from Nothing*. This book will help widen perspectives and narrow the differences between us. John is amazing and so inspiring, and the book is both well-timed and relevant."
—**Susie Buffett, Chair, The Sherwood Foundation**

"Full economic inclusion is an essential concept for an America that is currently fearful and fractured but never feckless. John Hope Bryant's prescription forecasts bringing this concept to life will yield a prognosis of enduring stability and sustainable prosperity. Read on and let's get to it."
—Lisa M. Borders, former Chair, The Coca-Cola Foundation

"This book arrived at the right moment in time, with the right stories for the right reason. It's beautifully written with a compelling perspective that establishes the case for optimism. We can all find our own reflection within these pages and be inspired to strive and thrive for ourselves and the greater good."
—Eduardo Martinez, President, The UPS Foundation, and Chief Diversity and Inclusion Officer, UPS

"This is a time when the world is uncertain and looks for pragmatic suggestions in order to chart viable livelihoods as we rebuild. Following the devastation caused by a global pandemic, it is reasonable that the right chosen voices rise to inspire us out of gloom.

"It is correct that a black man, whose entire heritage is underscored by immense physical hardship and emotional pain, should be the one we trust on our way to triumph. John Hope Bryant has proven again and again with his compassionate understanding of humanity and his sharp acumen that he is more than credible. This book is precisely the guide we need as a manual to help us navigate a way to greatness.

"He has illustrated the importance of proximity to greatness by quoting familiar figures who have been actively positive in our own business's growth. This evidences the power of owning our narrative and determines how the future frames us. He correctly calibrates our historic victories as a reference while challenging us to innovate and engineer new paths!"
—Lindo and Zondwa Mandela, Mandela Legacy Foundation

"John Bryant is both a force of nature and a force of good for this country. John has committed himself to helping those communities that have had less access to the American Dream. He works tirelessly to improve financial literacy, and his consistent efforts on economic empowerment, improved education for minority children, and access to attractively priced capital are admirable. Unfortunately, the world will not get better or more fair overnight, but it will get better over time if all of us take a moment to listen more carefully to many of John's recurring observations. John Bryant's goal is to push our country to acknowledge obvious inequalities and take the required steps to address them. It may not be easy, but it will be worthwhile—so I share John's goal and respect his passion for making the world a better place."
—Tony Ressler, cofounder and Executive Chairman, Ares Management Corp.

"John Bryant continues to challenge us all to be (and to do) better. His focus on personal accountability, a concept too often cast aside these days, provides an important reminder that all of us can and should take control of our own destiny. John is a living example that the American Dream lives on and can be achieved by all."

—Frank D. Martell, President and CEO, CoreLogic

"I want to offer up an amen to the powerful testimony that is my dear friend's new book, *Up from Nothing*. John shares masterfully and vulnerably the truth of his rise in business, philanthropy, stewardship, and education. Having lived what he teaches—some may even say preaches—every chapter of his life is a solid lesson in what it takes within ourselves and, importantly, as a nation to climb the ladder of success, to rise up together. John and I have never needed to research if we are blood related (though my mom suggests we most likely are), because we have always known we are of kindred minds and soul. We share the precious goal of giving forward without languishing in accusations about our pasts. Right now, for the first time in history, we are sharing the global goal of survival against a vicious pandemic, which makes John's book even more academically, spiritually, and universally relevant—and necessary. This book is a blessing to everyone no matter his or her station in life. It bears reading over and over . . . as I certainly shall."

—Janice Bryant Howroyd, founder and CEO, ActOne Group

UP FROM NOTHING

THE UNTOLD STORY OF HOW WE (ALL) SUCCEED

UP FROM NOTHING

JOHN HOPE BRYANT

with a Foreword by Ambassador Andrew Young

BK®

Berrett–Koehler Publishers, Inc.

Berrett-Koehler Publishers, Inc.
1333 Broadway, Suite 1000
Oakland, CA 94612-1921
Tel: (510) 817-2277
Fax: (510) 817-2278
www.bkconnection.com

ORDERING INFORMATION
QUANTITY SALES. Special discounts are available on quantity purchases by corporations, associations, and others. For details, contact the "Special Sales Department" at the Berrett-Koehler address above.
INDIVIDUAL SALES. Berrett-Koehler publications are available through most bookstores. They can also be ordered directly from Berrett-Koehler: Tel: (800) 929-2929; Fax: (802) 864-7626; www.bkconnection.com.
ORDERS FOR COLLEGE TEXTBOOK/COURSE ADOPTION USE. Please contact Berrett-Koehler: Tel: (800) 929-2929; Fax: (802) 864-7626.

Distributed to the US trade and internationally by Penguin Random House Publisher Services.

Berrett-Koehler and the BK logo are registered trademarks of Berrett-Koehler Publishers, Inc.

Printed in Canada

Berrett-Koehler books are printed on long-lasting acid-free paper. When it is available, we choose paper that has been manufactured by environmentally responsible processes. These may include using trees grown in sustainable forests, incorporating recycled paper, minimizing chlorine in bleaching, or recycling the energy produced at the paper mill.

Library of Congress Cataloging-in-Publication Data
NAMES: Bryant, John, 1966– author.
TITLE: Up from nothing : the untold story of how we (all) succeed / John Hope Bryant.
DESCRIPTION: First edition. | Oakland, CA : Berrett-Koehler Publishers, Inc., [2020] | Includes bibliographical references and index.
Identifiers: LCCN 2020019159 | ISBN 9781523090358 (hardcover) | ISBN 9781523090365 (adobe pdf) | ISBN 9781523090372 (epub)
SUBJECTS: LCSH: United States—Economic conditions—2009– | Success—United States | Capitalism—United States.
CLASSIFICATION: LCC HC106.84 .B79 2020 | DDC 650.10973—dc23
LC record available at https://lccn.loc.gov/2020019159

FIRST EDITION

26 25 24 23 22 21 20 | 10 9 8 7 6 5 4 3 2 1

Book producer and text designer: BookMatters; copyeditor: Kirsten Janene-Nelson; proofer: Janet Reed Blake; indexer: Leonard Rosenbaum; cover designer: Nita Ybarra

CONTENTS

To Breonna Taylor, Ahmaud Arbery, George Floyd, and the long list of others whose lives were taken, yet seen, so that finally, the story of the struggle for justice for Black America, in the United States of America, might finally be told. Our work as a nation now is to ensure not one of them died in vain.

We are not invisible. We are relevant. We do count. We all can contribute. All of us are America. This is our country together. Let's go.

FOREWORD

AMBASSADOR ANDREW YOUNG

Up *from Nothing* is a fascinating story, and John Hope Bryant really believes that it's not just his story, but it's the story available for all of us. It's how we all succeed.

If there ever was a time that America needed a giant push from the bottom of the pyramid—a massive creation of new ideas for new businesses, of new services, of new ways to expand our economy in the wake of this pandemic—this book is that push, and it is right on time. John makes it sound very easy, but I'm sure it was not ever easy for him. Nor will it be easy for any of the rest of us who are starting out at the bottom. But John is blessed with an unparalleled capacity of self-esteem and self-confidence, and I often wonder where it came from. In his book he gives most of the credit to his mother and father, but there are many mothers and fathers who bestow blessings upon their children without those children achieving similar results. There's something special about John Bryant, something I've been trying to figure out for almost twenty years.

John told me that he'd tried to engage me as a mentor

for almost ten years, starting in the late nineties, and that I'd seemed to have been avoiding him. He's probably right; the young people who we in the civil rights movement were looking for in the 1960s and 1970s were mostly young men and women who were willing to sacrifice even their lives for the freedom struggle. Whereas John had grown up in Los Angeles, specifically Compton, amid all of the racial pressures and tensions and police activity and police conflict, and I didn't sense that kind of sacrificial humility in him. But then, at a conference in South Africa, at a restaurant called the Back of the Moon, I witnessed John and Lance Triggs, dancing with two South African women, in a dance competition—and, wow, those brothers were good. I later learned that they had both come up through Don Cornelius's *Soul Train*, which had launched a cultural revolution in Black America. It takes a heck of a lot of confidence to dance down a soul train line every day, offering a different step or style and rhythm to a national audience. And so, for me, *Soul Train* completed the puzzle. Yes, John was curious, and confident, and ambitious, but there is a type of *self-esteem* that one develops in dance competitions in the hood. John seems to have taken his mother's love and support, mixed it with the encouragement of mentors from business, church, and City Hall, and blended it with that ghetto swag—creating quite a personality. And once I figured him out, I realized the extent to which he'd done something special and made it work. Not only in the fires of Watts, but also in the calm and reason of board rooms from Los Angeles to New York.

Now, everybody doesn't have to be a *Soul Train* dancer to be a success, but *dance* in African culture, like spirituals, gives you almost a direct connection between earth and heaven. I'm from New Orleans, and it's hard for me to imagine a God who has no rhythm, or an economy with no sense of swag. John's story describes his struggle with the social and economic realities of being born black in America. But, having no sense of inferiority or lack of confidence, he's been put to the test around the world and, somehow, anywhere he goes, they always invite him back.

This is a story well worth reading. It's a story that any young person of any race, creed, color, or agenda can learn much from. And it's a story that those who were born into success—and who now lead corporate America, and govern our cities and states, and occupy our national cabinet positions—will enjoy reading also. For this book offers a sense of the massive waves of talent struggling across our nation's streets and suites, trying to fulfill the American Dream. John has been blessed, and he's been lucky, but most of all he's been confident and determined to live out the true meaning of the American Dream. "We hold these truths to be self evident, that all men are created equal, that they are endowed by their Creator with certain unalienable Rights, that among these are Life, Liberty and…the *Pursuit* of Happiness." John loves the pursuit, and you will, too.

PREFACE

This is not a book about the pandemic, or the jobs crisis, or Black Lives Matter, or how to get more money, or about getting rich, or starting a business—but it's also about all of those things, ultimately. It's about your new winning mindset and about you winning in your lifetime. It's about reimagining a better way for us all to win.

As I write this Preface, in late spring of 2020, our nation is confronting the reality of the police brutality and other injustices that are a daily part of the African American experience, not to mention "lockdown" life with record unemployment claims and an uncertain future—without a functioning economy. What I see is an opportunity for a powerful, once-in-a century reset.

In many ways, the American Dream is falling into disrepair. Income and wealth inequality have reached unsustainable breach levels. Racial and political divisions have escalated to heights unseen in close to a century—defining us all more by what is separate and apart, rather than what binds us all together.

The international protests and civil unrest that followed

the murder of George Floyd at the hands of a white Minneapolis police officer are a clear example of the unattainability of the American Dream for certain groups in our country. Our justice and economic systems are broken. The murder of George Floyd and countless other black men and women by the police exemplify why Americans must focus on our unfinished business, not only so we can move forward, but so we can fulfill our greatest shared promises: Freedom. Self-determination. The American Dream...for all.

Another way our dream is failing is in how we have been treating our planet. We have let our environmental responsibility get away from us. The planet that we all live on, that we all share, is increasingly shedding, sometimes violently, unsustainable layers of its natural skin. I see on the other side of the growing Black Lives Matter movement and Coronavirus pandemic an opportunity for us all to take a collective deep breath, reassess our values—what we are about and what we are for—and to recast the business plan of America as one that is empowering and sustainable for all of us. It is clear to me that America has reached its "up from nothing" moment—and we can all agree that there is a lot of nothing to come up from for all of us. For America to succeed, we now need us to seize our moment as well.

This book is not about black and white, as in race, or red and blue, as in politics. This book is about the color green—as in money *and,* if you will, as in a more sustainable world—and it's about every stakeholder in America committing to forgetting the noise. This book is about how we stop messing with our own business plan so we can all come up;

how we rebuild a country that will sustain us all—culturally, financially, and environmentally—for the future. It's about recognizing the value of the invisible people at the bottom of the pyramid, about turning the barely surviving into thriving and us all being winners.

This book wants to blow up all the norms and hit RESET on the American Dream. It's time.

Everyone in the world seems to want to be Americans... except Americans. And this, my friends, is sad. We have got to get our belief back. Our optimism. Our business plan for a truly aspirational life. Our hope.

Forget all those isms—capitalism, socialism, racism—forget politics. This book is about US-ism. US as in you and me—all of us—and US as in the US of A. This book is about how we save ourselves from ourselves and keep on winning as a country.

I'm tired of stacked decks, aren't you?

Let's go. Together. To a place where all boats rise.

America's "Up from Nothing" Story

merica is a country with an ego, a bit of a chip on its
shoulder. At the dawning of this new nation, she had
something to prove to the world. I can relate. I too had something to prove, coming up from nothing in Compton, California, and South-Central Los Angeles. Up until recently, I
can admit that I still felt as if I had something to prove to the
world. Becoming reasonably comfortable in your own skin
comes with time, with both maturity and a long, hard search
for inner strength.

I also admit that, as an African American, a direct descendant of a brutally enslaved people brought here against their
will—enslaved, I might add, by many of the groups that I
will reference with detached admiration for their grit—it is
more than a little odd that I'm writing a book that says to set
aside, for the moment, the "noise" of racism, among other
things, in America.

But in many ways, my being the bearer of this message actually makes it more credible. Given my skin color, I have every good reason to wave away all the facts I will present here and instead focus on the legitimate anger and anguish I feel when I reflect on the history of my people in America. The injustices brought by slavery and racism are etched into the soul of my black community to this very day. You see its effects echoed in a kind of collective low self-esteem, in a lack of real confidence and belief in the system of mainstream success, and, worst of all, in lost hope.

But there are countless great scholars who have already chronicled those sickening injustices far better than I ever could. And, more so, adding my voice to that chorus would not make fixing the problem today one ounce easier. Sometimes, focusing on the pain just makes it feel worse. Last, this book is not about my feelings. This is a book about building (rebuilding) a nation of winners from every corner of the race and economic spectrum, especially the African American corner.

So instead I am focusing on how to take the good about America and make it work for us all. I want us all to fix our problem, starting right where we stand, by signing up, maybe for the first time ever, for the same team. America has succeeded *in spite of* our many glaring shortcomings. But what if we eliminated some of those shortcomings—like our absurd focus on race, and our broken aspirational ladder for those at the bottom? What would happen if we had a business plan that focused on what we're *for* (as in winning) rather than what we're *against* (as in each other)?

Back in its earliest days, the young upstart country calling itself the United States of America did not have royalty, or the class-oriented bloodlines of Europe, or the vaulted history of the Middle East, or the large populations of China, India, or Africa. She hit RESET on all that noise about what it takes to win as a nation. And she turned necessity into opportunity.

America turned to her immigrated, otherwise-written-off upstarts to create its own class structure—with entrepreneurs and business owners at the top. Celebrity, a uniquely American creation, became our own form of royalty, with a small *r*.

Let me explain the American success story in the most straightforward way possible: America is the largest economy in the world because she is not actually a country, she is an idea. And that idea is freedom. Freedom of opportunity for all (almost). And that's where our opportunity today lies.

As I'm finishing the writing of this book, I'm sheltering at home here in Atlanta, Georgia, doing my part to flatten the curve as the COVID-19 virus sweeps through every state in our country, shattering every idea we had about how we live, work, and prosper.

It's like the universe is sending us a message to reset.

What if we took America's dream of freedom for *almost* all and made sure it was accessible to actually every American, regardless of race, color, background, and gender?

What if we grabbed this opportunity to rebuild America into a nation where we all can win? That's what I'm writing about.

❖   ❖   ❖

The early Americans who volunteered to come here were a hodge-podge collection of assertive, type-A personalities from all over the world: first from England, Ireland, Italy, Germany, Poland, and so many other places, and later from Africa, Latin America, and Asia. These are the people who helped create the aspirational new America we know today, and it is they who I will discuss first. I will address the very different stories of the Native American and enslaved African populations in due time.

It is worth noting that most of the peoples in all of these places stayed right where they were. And understandably so. Coming to America for these early immigrants was a crazy gamble. They came to America from 6,000 or more miles away, with the equivalent of $50 in their pockets, armed with nothing more than a dream to become something. They took a huge gamble because they were crazy enough to believe in themselves and in America. They believed that America was their opportunity to come up from nothing.

America thrived because most of her people were the type to leave behind the comforts of home and all they knew in search of something more. They were hooked on a dream of aspirational opportunity. They were hooked on freedom.

You know the story. They came here through Ellis Island, looked up, and said, "I'm going to live the American Dream for me and my family. With *no* money, and no sponsor. Just a dream and grit."

Now, either these people were criminally insane or they were geniuses waiting to be tapped and mined. Certainly they had an unmined, unproven belief in their own future success. They were winners who hadn't even won yet.

These individuals possessed the qualities that I believe make America exceptional:

- ▶ They were hooked on freedom and making their own way on their own terms.

- ▶ They had a capacity for reinvention. They didn't want where they came from to matter as much as where they were going.

- ▶ They had up-from-nothing grit, an "I am all I need to make it happen" attitude toward success and life.

These type-A personalities believed in America as the only place where they could reinvent themselves, make their own way on their own terms, be free. As for me, I am not sure that my bottom-to-the-top story would have been possible in any place but America—race limitations and discrimination factors included.

America is the only place where the belief in yourself is enough to succeed, to create the future you seek. Everywhere else, you have to believe in something else—like a king, or a social system. In America, we have the freedom and opportunity to determine our own success.

This book is about possibilities. The only question is, do you believe?

America, the Green

The new color for America is green—and yet it's also always been green.

Not white, black, red, brown, or yellow, as in race. Not red or blue, as in partisan politics.

Green, as in the color of US currency.

Are there race and racism issues in America? That's like asking if rain is real. Yes, of course there are. My black ancestors were absolutely limited by and because of racism. To a lesser degree, I have been too. Racism was at the base of slavery and the slave trade in America—but what was underneath that base was money and economics. Slave labor was a wealth-building tool, the building of wealth on the literal backs of others. Africans weren't enslaved only because Europeans saw them as an inferior race; Africans were brought to America because they were agricultural geniuses with an insane work ethic, even under the most extreme conditions.

Let me include the talk about politics here too. Of course politics are important. Many of our greatest wins for both the mainstream and the underserved have been achieved through the political narrative. But underneath politics, and driving it, is money and economics. War too. No country goes to war "just" to save a country of poor people. It's all too often, more like 95 percent of the time, about that country's economic relevance.

So let's not get into a side-tracked, emotional argument about and around race or politics here, because those induce anger. This is how they get you: they take you off track, they distract you, they make you unfocused and emotional.

Complaining about our reality is not going to get our kids into college. Complaining is not a business plan; in fact, it messes with our business plan. For what it's worth, payback is not a business plan either. Reparations are absolutely needed, but by themselves reparations are not how we will win. We need to get our priorities right. Let's put our focus back on the green.

My billionaire businessman friend and partner Tony Ressler taught me something about business, life, and social change. In a private moment, he acknowledged what we all know but don't like to say.

"John, of course racism is real, and it's horrible. That said, you cannot change the way someone feels about you. The way you can achieve social justice today—the way a generation of black America can achieve social justice today—is probably a combination of as much education as you can handle, access to capital, and access to opportunity, at scale. Success, and a little money in your pocket (let's call that wealth creation), goes a long way to leveling the playing field. This is how you can help your people."

Tony later suggested that we work together to build a generation of successful entrepreneurs from the sections of our economy that have been left behind—and that is in part why I wrote this book.

This book is disruptive. Positively disruptive, yes, but it is no doubt disruptive. Intentionally disruptive. Not intentionally irritating or argumentative. Intellectually, culturally, and spiritually disruptive.

Getting everybody in America up from nothing is about a higher consciousness, a higher-frequency thinking. And it's about action.

The message of this book is for every stakeholder in America to start thinking beyond the racism and politics that plague our airwaves, because they only serve to divide us. The message of this book is US-ism—how everyone in America can turn our attention back to our winning business plan. This book is selfish; it's also about our sustained uplift as a nation.

The greatness of America rests within the will, spirit, and determination of its people. This greatness is as old as the country's founding itself. It was reflected in our independence from Britain, our civil war, our civil rights movement (which was not just about black people—it just unfortunately starred us), our domination of arts and culture, and our history of economic builders. Our greatness lies in our striving to be great, to succeed globally, and to accomplish things that no other nation has accomplished in the history of the modern world.

It's important for us to know that we can succeed—that we have succeeded, literally up from nothing.

We need to change the way we see ourselves—not as survivors or even thrivers, but as winners. And we need to change the way we see others—not as enemies or, worse yet, irrelevant, but as essential parts of our collective up-from-nothing story.

Consider this: Why should a racist CEO want his minority employee base to have everything to succeed and live a good life? Because if they succeed, he does.

We cannot segregate our hearts and integrate our wallets. Coming up together is the business plan for America— where everyone rises, and everyone can win. This is how we actually make America great again.

You can do it. We all can do it. News flash: We all *have* to do it.

And let me tell you something else: there are countries that are hoping that we don't do it, that we forget how we ever did it in the first place.

CHAPTER 1

What We Forgot about the American Dream

W hat if I told you that there was a cancer in America more destructive than racism? A problem of intent more harmful than hate? What if I told you that the real issue in America today was increasingly not love or hate, but indifference. Or worse, radical indifference. People—a group of powerful and wealthy people even—who don't care enough about you to even hate you.

The biggest problem in America today, the reason for all the destructive divisions among us, is that we have forgotten our storyline. We have forgotten how we got here, how we succeeded, and what it takes to sustain that same level of success. For the last two-hundred-plus years, America has been winning because of the spiritual wealth of her people, and because of our great belief in America as the Land of Opportunity.

Today we are facing the cancer of spiritual poverty. We

have lost our belief in our ability to win. We have lost our storyline.

On an individual level, getting your mind right is the single most important thing you can do to get your life right. You've got to commit yourself, every day of your life, to removing the old, bad, negative, destructive tapes from your mind, and replacing them with new, positive ones. It is literally true that whether you believe that you can, or believe that you can't, you're right. (Thanks for that one, Henry Ford.)

Unfortunately, in America today it seems like half the country is suffering from some form of depression. And this is a problem, because belief is the most basic requirement of an aspirational mindset, of a thriving or winning state of mind, and it stands at the door of any positive action.

Our Own Worst Enemy

While it is no doubt true that social and economic mobility has become a real problem for the average worker, America is still one of very few places where you can literally start at the bottom of the ladder and then own the ladder twenty to thirty years later.

The untapped, unleveraged opportunity for America's future is her next generation of GDP growers. Rebuilding the ladder for certain groups who have been historically disenfranchised is our shared potential opportunity.

Today, as an example, only 2 percent of all businesses in America with one employee or more are owned by African Americans.[1] Where would we be (we, as in America, the country), if the roadblocks hindering African Americans were removed?

Today, African Americans—this proud and deserving race of people—have just about 10 percent of the net worth of their white counterparts. This is not me throwing shade or starring in my own whining session; this is me saying we are all acting like idiots. We are idiots for holding *any* people back. We are idiots for focusing on how to cut up a smaller economic pie instead of growing and sharing a larger pie among us all.

For hundreds of years, America systematically stole black lives, black freedom, and black labor. It was a theft of labor and a reverse transfer of wealth enshrined in law and enforced by violence. Do you know when the word "millionaire" was coined? Circa 1850, to describe the (white) amassers of huge wealth in the wealthiest city per capita in the world, in Natchez, Mississippi, a center of trade (and slave trade) in the South. There were a whole lot of cotton fields along the Mississippi River back then...What kind of labor do you think was working them?

Black slavery is literally how we birthed our country's first millionaires.

The impact of this theft over a period of centuries has meant an enormous loss of wealth for individuals and families across generations—a kind of compound interest in reverse.

It's time to say enough—and to do something about it! It's time to stop being idiots.

On Martin Luther King Jr. Day in 2020, billionaire

Michael Bloomberg spoke to the people of Tulsa, Oklahoma, and lay down this bombshell: "We can decide to invest in black wealth creation. And just think about this: if we could eliminate the racial wealth gap in this generation, we would add $1.5 trillion to the economy."[2]

He didn't say anything here about charity or handouts. He was suggesting that, by creating future wealth for those previously left behind, we can bridge the economic wealth gap in our generation *and* generate an extra $1.5 trillion in GDP—creating a larger economic pie to pass around.

That's a hand up, not a handout. And it pays a dividend too.

Here's a story about what happens when people choose to play nice (spoiler: they win together).

Operation HOPE, Inc., is a nonprofit, for-purpose organization working to disrupt poverty. We do this primarily by providing financial literacy empowerment and economic education to low- and moderate-income youth and adults. When I founded Operation HOPE in Los Angeles back in 1992, no one really knew what I was talking about. Financial literacy was far from a common topic. Not many showed up for that first meeting, where I shared my vision for a city emerging from the ashes of the Rodney King riots—and of those who did, not many believed. But those who attended left believing that I believed, and that alone was enough to hold Operation HOPE together during those first five rocky years or so.

All of this tenacity, resiliency, and refusal to give up, along with my absolute obsession with winning and becoming the person in the room who could not be denied—on merit, substance, or delivering tangible results—all of this led directly to the founding of Operation HOPE.

Around the same time that I started Operation HOPE, Mayor Tom Bradley had asked businessman and noted civic leader Peter Ueberroth to launch what became known as Rebuild Los Angeles (RLA). It immediately raised tens of millions of committed dollars and recruited the city's best leaders to come on board pro bono or in loaned executive capacities. Of course, it also had the mayor's, and thus the city's, imprimatur. It became *the* center of response and the official resource point for all things related to the rebuilding of the city.

I loved everything about it. I did not see RLA as any kind of competition to my efforts; I saw it as an enhancement. There were enough poverty and problems to solve to go around. I welcomed with open arms the credibility that RLA provided to all of our community efforts, even if it limited the resources flowing directly to my fledgling organization. I believe this is where I adopted the philosophy that 10 percent of something big was much better than 90 percent or even 100 percent of something small. I was not ego-tripping; I was trying to create scale and impact. I'm basically in the same exact business today.

But the vast majority of other nonprofit leaders in the community I spoke to resented RLA and what it represented: the centralization of substantial resources. Most other community-based nonprofits viewed RLA as competition; as a result, they did not go out of their way to help RLA or anyone associated with them. Not only did I want to help RLA, I lobbied anyone and everyone I knew to join their board! And I stepped up too, becoming the youngest member of the RLA board of directors.

I supported RLA because we shared the same mission. But it's also true that I benefited hugely from the association. Actually, RLA was such a good idea that I borrowed several pages out of its book, including the partnership model of the private sector, government, and community all working together. This is a critical element of the HOPE business plan, and without question I got this from RLA. And while RLA never made a direct grant to Operation HOPE or sent any funding directly our way, Operation HOPE and I absolutely benefited from the association and the relationship capital. We both gave and received.

I ended up with a major pro bono law firm commitment through someone I met at RLA. I built relationships with several major corporate leaders, including Peter Ueberroth, who ended up staking me at many critical junctures. In fact, there is no doubt in my mind that Peter Ueberroth was continually a key "Now, who is this guy again?" credibility call when VIPs wanted to check me out. Like when I invited President George W. Bush to visit South-Central Los Angeles on the tenth anniversary of the riots. There is no doubt in my mind that the White House handlers called Peter, among others, to vouch for me. He vouched for my character, which he has done since I was twenty-six and continues to do to this day.

But, unfortunately, despite Peter's brilliant vision for community revitalization and change, RLA was doomed from the beginning. That was because his nonprofit was a political creation, and so for every one who wanted it to succeed, there were two who actively conspired for it to fail. There were a number of cochairs of RLA representing different constituency groups throughout the city. Basically, it was an organizational mess, and that is part of why RLA never worked—because it was a house divided. In late 1992 or mid 1993, when I saw that RLA was starting to be blamed for even the faltering of the Los Angeles Unified School District, I knew their days were numbered. Of course, RLA had no power over the city's school district. This was politics.

Infighting within RLA became so pervasive there was often little time to get any real business done. From this I learned to remove myself from the noise, and to focus like a laser beam on producing tangible results. I also began to learn how to get out of my own way. One of the cochairs, Bernard Kinsey—a retired Xerox executive and the only African American in leadership at RLA and in on the rebuilding effort back then—pulled me into an office one day and gave me some advice that I use to this day. He had heard me go on and on and on with my vision for rebuilding the city. He said, "John, don't use twenty words when two will do!" I took it to heart. Busy people don't have the time or interest in hearing me drone. I learned to cut to the chase.

It's great that I learned all I did, because back then pretty much everyone counted out me and Operation HOPE. In

1994 I won a bank grant for $600,000—my entire annual operating budget. When I went to pick up the check I was told the grant request had been sent back to committee at the bank. Translation: Someone had convinced them to not give it to me. It hurt me to my core, but I got over it.

It didn't kill me; it made me more resilient. It made me harder to kill. And I learned that I had to dial back my utter, absolute optimism to a level of passion and emotional engagement that my audience could handle. I had to learn how to funnel my passion into two words rather than twenty. They could only handle, say, 30 percent of me, and yet I was giving them 100 percent. I just overwhelmed whomever I was talking to. I spooked them, and they ran for the doors.

And soon after that, I got a call from a city official who was on my first founding board of directors. He instructed me to change my letterhead from "eradicating poverty in America," to "eradicating poverty [exclusively in his local district]." I refused. He threatened to resign from my board. I still refused. He resigned. His resignation letter made its way to the funding office of yet another planned early donor, who also pulled back their commitment. This was a plan, consciously or unconsciously, to bury me. I was an irritant. I would not play ball. I could not be controlled. I was a problem. I had to go. Well, I just decided to ignore it all.

What it taught me was this important life lesson: learn to go through life consciously oblivious to most things around you. Be ruthless about how you and others use your time.

Stay focused on things that matter—and ignore all the rest. I put my head down into my own optimistic rabbit hole of hope and just moved forward. By the time I lifted my head, Operation HOPE had emerged as the only post–Rodney King riots nonprofit organization to go national, yet alone to expand beyond the city and state.

The Dream Is Alive; the Ladder Is Broken

Pretend for a moment that it's possible to take racism and racial issues out of the disgusting business of both the slave trade and slavery itself. What it actually was at its core was the largest reverse generational wealth transfer in modern history—not to mention bad capitalism.

When I say this, I am not trying to make an emotional statement, or an anger statement, or a reparations statement. Nor am I even remotely attempting a guilt trip. I have only one, nonemotional point to make: the thing that helped every honest, and even dishonest, entrant to the American experience was their own self-determination. They were individuals benefiting from their own industriousness, allowed to reap the returns of their own hard work and the sweat of their brows. And yet, this opportunity for self-determination was 100 percent denied to African American "immigrants" for more than 300 years.

Let's put this into proper context. The complete American experiment is a little over 450 years in total, and slavery represented approximately 300 years of that history. African

Americans spent 300 years enslaved, and 150 years free—
but at least 100 of those post-slavery "free" years functioned
within a system that we refer to as "Jim Crow," which is basically just another name for economic and social repression.

So we're talking about a group of people who for over 400
years in America had no meaningful chance of benefiting
from what most proudly refer to as the "sweat of their brow,"
their natural smarts, or their raw intellectual genius. None
of what they were born with or developed was theirs to keep.

As part of Reconstruction, on March 3rd, 1865, President
Abraham Lincoln founded Freedman's Bank "to support the
land grants and other elements of the Freedman's Bureau
Act," and "help newly freed Americans navigate their financial lives."[3] By 1874, that venture had completely failed. That
fact makes clear that there was never a broad-based effort
to make sure that African Americans had even the most
basic financial literacy. No one attempted to teach them how
money, banking, entrepreneurship, small business creation,
and big business growth work.

We live in a free enterprise democracy in America—
indeed, the nation was founded on that basis—but no one
has ever made it a priority to ensure that African Americans
had even the most basic clue of what it meant to succeed in
that environment.

And so, mainstream America directly benefited from
the wealth created by the tireless efforts of industrious and
hard-working blacks, who were 100 percent unpaid for three
centuries. The agricultural economy rocketed growth in
early America, rooted as it was in that wealth accumulation

in land—lots of it—much of it fertile farmland worked with free slave labor.

White America smartly took their accumulated wealth creation and cashflow, now spilling forth from the agricultural age, and moved to protect their wealth (and way of life in the American South) by taking up positions in public service. They became high-ranking elected officials to protect what they and others had built. You could say the success of white America began and ended with wealth creation—except the wealth creation didn't end; it just got larger. After they left office, ninety-nine times out of one hundred, it was back to business for them. It became a well-known circular route for my mainstream friends that began and ended with wealth creation.

For black America, post the achievement of their physical freedom, the mainstream route to success was religion and church, general education and community good, civil rights, social justice, politics and political office, and then—for most—a good job. The prize for black America, ninety-nine times out of one hundred, was a good job. More times than not, we were the ones cashing checks, not writing them. Making money, yes; but building wealth—not so much.

The route to success for white America was specialized education, then business ownership, to wealth, to politics, back to wealth, and even more business creation.

The route to success for the main of black America was mostly civil society in nature. World War II created a level playing field for trained black professionals, and what emerged was a generation of black doctors and nurses, lawyers and accountants, and other skilled professions. The one and noteworthy exception to this rule, which has helped to create real wealth for some, was black America's incredible and outsized achievement in professional sports and the arts. And even this success ties back to our slave journey. Our art emerged from our strong church tradition. Our athletic achievement emerged from the expression of the only asset we had partial control over: our own bodies.

And the math makes sense here as well, because if you look at African American achievement in these two master-class spaces, you can recognize immediately that (1) the rules were published, and (2) the playing field was level. And so we excelled. We were winners.

If you sang or danced or played an instrument well, you were a winner, and you won—period. If you ran fast, or jumped high, or swung the bat like no one else ever had, then you dominated the game, and you won. You were a winner. But the problem here is that these two master-class areas of professional achievement and wealth creation are narrow and extremely limited pathways to success. We're talking about hundreds of jobs and positions of wealth creation, maybe a few thousand every year—when what we need are pathways for millions.

Despite black America's brilliance, talent, and industriousness, we never got what I call "the memo" on real, broad-based, sustained business and wealth creation. White America owned that memo—and they owned it from the first inning of the first game.

Now, to be totally clear, what I'm laying out here is not an indictment of all (or most) white people of that era. There are many positive examples of these *same* mainstream white members of the wealthy class, the power structure, who used their wealth and power to free slaves, to grant safe passage for the unjustly persecuted, and to provide real opportunity to black Americans.

The founding backers of the Freedman's Bank were enlightened white elites. The founders of the National Association for the Advancement of Colored People (NAACP), and the National Urban League, were a thoughtful collection of enlightened blacks and whites who worked together and put their lives at risk in order to create institutions that America needed then and still needs now. These and other examples of powerful white men and women, in and out of business, in and out of the community, and in and out of politics, are legend, and they deserve to be recognized and acknowledged. But none of this is the point.

My nonemotional point here is about the system itself, and the accepted culture that produced that unequitable system. The system has never worked for African Americans—nor has it worked for many other groups. The business plan for America was all messed up. In some ways, it still is.

Again, I am not talking about the exceptions. I am talking here about the rule. The rule whipped black America's aspirational rear end from sunup to sundown, every day, while rewarding even the most average of their mainstream counterparts. This is the math of the matter. This is my point.

When people think about affirmative action, people automatically think about black people. But actually, the first beneficiaries of affirmative action were my white brothers and sisters. Twice. See above for the first example: three-hundred-plus years of unequal access to the uniquely American aspirational dream, plus the rules to achieve it.

The second experience of affirmative action for white people immediately followed World War II. It was called the G.I. Bill. Now, let me make it clear that I think this was a brilliant move for America. Ensuring that every returning American military veteran from World War II got as much education as they could consume, a down payment for a home they could own, and an apprenticeship for a well-paying job was how we created what we now call the American middle class.

To this day, the agricultural business sector (read: 99 percent mainstream farmers in rural America) are the recipients of literally the largest financial and economic subsidy, year after year, in America's history.[4]

Why do we do it? Our leaders will tell you that it is in America's interest.

Well, this book is designed to convince the reader that imagining new strategies to support the unleveraged talents, hopes, and aspirations of the rest of left-behind America—which is not just American blacks by the way—is also in America's interest, and always has been.

African Americans are absolutely not the only group that has been left behind in America, but let me use them as an example one more time. Bridging the wealth gap for black America alone would create trillions—that's with a *t*—of additional GDP and American wealth. The color of those trillions isn't black, though. It's green, and it benefits us all.

Capitalism Still Wins

Even if you want to distribute money like a socialist, you first have to collect money, like a capitalist.

—THE LATE SHIMON PERES, speaking to John Hope Bryant, encouraging him to "keep going" with Operation HOPE

Ownership is a big deal, and an ownership mentality might be an even bigger deal. When individuals do not see themselves as owners of something, they treat that thing differently.

No one washes rental cars. The nicest people in the world don't wash rental cars. They rent the car, drive it—until the wheels come off, even—let the dirt accumulate until they could write WASH ME on the windows, and then at the end of the rental contract they return the car to the car owner, possibly with no gas in the tank.

Likewise, the worker, disconnected from their employer and employment-engagement experience, may take on the destructive productivity perspective of "in late, long lunch, leave early." In other words: indifference. Treading water. Just barely showing up. Giving minimal effort. Basic compliance. The problem is that this attitude, approach, and perspective never made anything great, anywhere.

In the twentieth century, worker's unions emerged as a means to level the playing field for the average American, to provide them with the first-ever worker's rights. Leaders in free enterprise and capitalism also weighed in with their own creative solutions, such as Ford founder Henry Ford's bold effort to pay his workers double their former pay, helping to create the new American middle class in the process.

But the twenty-first century saw an increasingly widening income, wealth, and opportunity gap in America. This new challenge has inspired highly intelligent, thoughtful, and otherwise very reasonable people to talk down capitalism and the free enterprise system in exchange for a socialist one.

This attraction to socialism is understandable. So many feel that the current system has failed them and believe it will fail their children as well. But socialism is not sustainable. An overwhelming majority—90 percent—of the world's nations that switched to a socialist (or worse still, a communist) model over the past two hundred years has failed. In fact, the two most prominent examples of communist societies, China and Russia, have—oddity beyond oddity—chosen the Western capitalist model as their own.

As it happens, what most people laud as successful socialism is really free enterprise with a progressive tax scheme attached. Nordic countries like Sweden aren't truly socialist. Anyone there can start a business, build it, make a lot of money, and create wealth. The deal there is just that the government requires you pay taxes of half or more of your income, which it then uses to take care of the state—health care, public education, providing a safety net for the poor, and everything else. The people in these countries obviously think this is a great deal for them, and I applaud them for that. But this also means that the government is the babysitter, the minder, and the "educator" of the poor. With the best of intentions, the government is both preventing those at the bottom from falling between the cracks (the good part), and preventing them from ever rising up and climbing onto their own roofs—let alone building a second or third story on their own (the bad part). It's not because the government doesn't want the poor to rise (they probably do), but because they can't. How can the government possibly teach someone how to come up from nothing—as entrepreneurs and self-made builders of business—when they haven't done that themselves? When there are no aspirational models in the culture? This is not a criticism, it's just an *is*. Like I like to say, "It's what you don't know that you don't know but that you think you know that's killing you."

I fully believe that if I had been born in France, a country I love for many reasons, I would not have become who I am in the world today. If I had been born in Japan, which I love also; or the UK, with all of its benefits; or Germany, where I have connections tied to my knighthood from the noble class there; or Norway, one of the happiest and healthiest places in the world; or the amazing African continent, or Latin America, or the Middle East—all great places I have visited—I would never have become who I am today, my own up-from-nothing story.

In fairness, most all of these places have done a better job than the United States has over the past fifty-plus years on the issue of basic social and economic mobility (moving from the poor class, to the working class, to the middle class),[5] but not one of them could have catapulted me from the inner cities of Compton and South-Central Los Angeles to the world stage, working peer to peer with billionaires, captains of industry, and heads of state. Nowhere but the United States combines 100 percent free enterprise, with 100 percent free-dom of opportunity (relatively speaking), with 100 percent freedom. No country produces winners from the whole cloth of absolutely nothing like America does.

I am passionate about the freedom part of our story. America—even with all of our drama and challenges and racism and inequality—was clearly the path for me. I saw that a free enterprise environment and a capitalist system hooked on freedom was the path of least resistance to the full expression of my God-given potential in this world. For me, America spelled "winning."

Now, socialism, on the other hand, could never have garnered me my wins. People in a socialist society don't own anything, and an ownership mentality is how we win.

God gave us two ears and one mouth so that we listen twice as much as we talk. So I love to listen and to learn everywhere that I go. I love listening to and speaking to waiters and taxi cab and Uber drivers whenever I find myself in their company. One day I had the pleasure of spending time with a highly educated Cuban gentleman at the restaurant where he worked in Chicago. I asked him about the Cuban socialist model, and at first he bragged extensively about a first-rate, free educational system that served all Cubans. Then I pressed him for additional information.

The gentleman shared with me that he was an engineer back in Cuba, but the nation was having a heck of a time finding any educated young people to take over his and similar skilled jobs there. Why? Because smart young people educated in the free Cuban system didn't much care for the idea that, no matter how hard they worked, someone or a group of someones right next to them, working half or one-quarter as hard, would receive the exact same pay. Or worse, those others could be promoted, regardless of whether they were qualified or had worked hard and earned better treatment and considerations. And so, an entire generation of young Cubans, educated for free in the Cuban system, simply left.

Where did they go? America, of course, where one's abilities and skilled effort could be and would be rewarded by the free enterprise system. This is the real story of the many waves of immigrants from all over the world that flooded into America for one reason: freedom of opportunity.

Today, fewer Americans are seeing the possibility of freedom of opportunity. An estimated 40 percent of current jobs will shrink or disappear over the next ten years.[6] Those still working today feel like they are getting less consideration for more and more effort and hard work. They've lost their aspirations because the model of aspirational success in America is broken.

I am seeking to change all of that. With this book, with our national ground game efforts through Operation HOPE and my other philanthropic, public sector, and thought-leadership efforts, I plan to reset the field.

It's time to remember some things about America and to reimagine some other things. The beauty is that America is not a country, she is an idea—and we can imagine and reimagine her to be anything we like.

It's time to remember our storyline, the original dream

for America: where you come from and what you look like doesn't matter as much as where you're going.

It's time to reimagine capitalism in a way that makes free enterprise work for all of God's children. It's time for a collective mental upgrade to create the America that she was always intended to be: the place that winners everywhere in the world want to find their way to, so they can secure for themselves that elusive thing we call freedom.

Russia and China Get It

Everyone wants to be an American—except Americans, that is. Russia and China want to eat our lunch. Russia and China want to be America. Or worse still, they want to beat America.

Why, you ask? Because they want our way of life, that's why. The very thing they attack, pretty much daily, is the very thing they don't have and crave: our freedoms and our global success.

Even with all of our problems—and, my God, there are countless of them—and regardless of what anyone else has said or says today, America is a special place. That's why it is still the sole superpower in the world today.

But here is the problem: others see America as special too, and they don't like this fact. It stands in the way of their progress, of their success. And so, they have to find ways to deconstruct us, to destroy us from the inside out. And the easiest way to destroy us is not to actually attack us—it is to somehow convince us that we are each other's enemy.

Make no mistake about it, China and Russia are at war with America. Right now. But smartly, they have chosen a better way to fight against us than bombs and bullets. After all, if they succeed in physically destroying us, it also destroys them too. America's success is inextricably linked to the long-term success of both Russia and China. Our economics are helplessly intertwined.

Their war on America is a war of divide and control, and it is leveraged with money, perverted self-interest, economic selfishness, and economic short-termism. The efforts of Russia's influence in our political system and our democracy is so obvious that I believe even my friend Stevie Wonder can see it (and yes, Stevie would find this joke amusing).

And China could not be more obvious of its intent. They have practically said it out loud. It is underscored every time they steal one of our countless legally protected intellectual property rights and make it their own—stealing it, effectively, in broad daylight. Or how they have used the power of their wallet to push around American democracy, to have us pawn our freedoms. Like when in October 2019 Daryl Morey, general manager of the NBA (National Basketball Association), stood up for basic freedoms and human dignity by tweeting support for Hong Kong protestors[7] only to have China attempt to bully, push, prod, intimidate, and crush his voice—simply because they believed that they could. And we almost fell for it.

But make no bones about it, China and Russia are testing our limits. Our inner fortitude. Our resolve. Our resiliency. They are working to figure out what we are really willing to stand for and, conversely, what we are willing to possibly sell ourselves for. And they are convinced that there is a price.

China is convinced that there is a price for everyone because, unfortunately, depressed human beings without a spiritual grounding are shockingly simple creatures, and our disconnect from our collective concern is an easy button to push.

A house divided cannot stand. It was true in biblical times and it's true now. The way we have been focusing on our differences has not only been messing with our business plan, it has been playing into the hands of China and Russia. And the one thing I know is that is not how we win. That is nobody's American Dream.

CHAPTER 2

The Thrivers and the Winners

At the beginning of 2020, I traveled to Arthur, Illinois—Amish and Mennonite country—to share the work and vision of Operation HOPE and our HOPE Inside model of community uplift. We had partnered with investment firm giant KKR & Co. to bring financial well-being coaching to line employees of the C.H.I. Overhead Doors company. For me, this was confirmation that our strategy for empowering black and brown people who have been traditionally left behind could work for our working class white brothers and sisters too. More than three-quarters of the employees wanted to sign up for the financial coaching and financial well-being work we do.

I spoke before an audience that was 95 percent working class white, rural, and nothing like me on the surface—and yet we had a lot in common. Even the gentleman sitting in the third row with the red MAKE AMERICA GREAT AGAIN hat nodded in agreement with me. After I spoke, countless employees approached me, sharing how my story sounded so much like their own. They wanted to know if I could help them to "come up" too.

Over the twenty-eight years since I founded Operation HOPE, my work has reinforced for me that financial well-being is not a white issue, a black issue, or a brown issue. It is neither a Republican issue (even though several in the audience demonstratively wore red "MAGA" hats) nor a Democratic issue. It is a green issue. My experience in Arthur, Illinois, didn't surprise me. None of this surprised me. It was simply more confirmation that we were on the right track.

What did shock me, though, was the kind of help these workers wanted from me. These hard-working, salt-of-the-earth, authentic, and now openly vulnerable employees spoke about how important it was to have the right attitude about life. The mental game. They wanted to find a way to be positive, to see solutions. Yes, they wanted our coaches' help with their finances, but they wanted my help with mindset. They wanted a mental, emotional, intellectual, and, if you will, a spiritual software upgrade of sorts. With that they knew they would begin to reimagine what their lives could be and what they could achieve.

Person after person after person told me how important they knew it was to get their heads right, so to speak. The thing that stood out to them the most was a story I'd shared asking what kind of bird they wanted to be: an eagle, a buzzard, or a turkey. They all wanted to be eagles.

I had told the audience that eagles don't fly in packs and

they always fly high. You never see a flock of eagles. They are high-altitude birds. They even raise their children differently. An eagle's nest is made of sharp little twigs. The message: when you get big enough that you're pushing up against the inside of that nest, well then it's time for you to get up and leave your parents' home. Go look after yourself. Get a job.

Buzzards, on the other hand, love packs. They are low-altitude birds. They prey and they scavenge. They are those people who are always standing on other people's heads in an effort to elevate themselves. Always player-hating, never player-congratulating. Always with something negative to say about somebody.

And then you have turkeys. Turkeys have wings and can't even fly. And before you become the cynic that shouts out, "But turkeys *can* fly!," let me explain that I am not talking about thirty feet off of the ground for fifty yards, so stop it, please. And this is sort of the point. Turkeys are profilers, loud mouths, cynics, and complainers. They're trying to be something they are not.

So at the end of my speech I asked the assembled employees, "What kind of bird do you want to be?" "Eagles!" they replied. As I walked through the warehouse after my talk, several different groups shouted enthusiastically in my direction, "I'm an eagle!"

It's like they found their own voices, maybe, just maybe, for the very first time. This is not a statement about me but about themselves, about how they saw themselves, maybe for the first time. This was mental reconditioning at its best.

In my talk I had described how the word "capital" comes from the Latin root word *capitale*, or "knowledge in the head." In other words, capital at its core is not about money but about mentality, a knowledge base, a perspective and way of seeing the world.

I have often said that mentality and your mental conditioning, your outlook on life, is everything. I cannot guarantee you that having a positive attitude will bring you to thrive. But what I can absolutely guarantee is that having a negative attitude will cause you to fail. Being negative is a business recipe for both near-term and long-term disaster.

The Thriving Mindset

The thriving mindset is what in many ways defines mainstream American aspiration today. It's about an education, opportunity, family structure, support, and stability (for you and your family). It's about making a life—generally speaking—getting a good job, and "cashing those checks." It's about making money and getting paid.

This approach to life first raised its head as the structural norm sometime after World War I, with Henry Ford creating what we refer to as the middle class today. He paid his workers enough to buy the automobiles they were making on the assembly line.

Thriving is a wonderful place to be, and most people I knew growing up dreamed about graduating into this place and space. The greatest symbol of this achievement is what today we refer to as the vaulted American Dream of the

American middle class. It has in many ways defined our standards of living in modern America today.

But there is another mindset altogether, what I refer to as a "winning mindset," and this is about building. It is about building a life, not just living one. It is about writing your own checks, not just cashing the checks others gave you. It is about creating wealth, not just getting paid. This is the mindset that built America.

The Winning Mindset

Whenever I have gone to an Atlanta Hawks basketball game with my friend Tony Ressler, owner of the team, Tony would sit in the third or fourth row of the stadium. He left the fancy seats and private suites for paying customers. He didn't wear the accoutrements of success that many of his players did. Tony wore plain jeans, a colored shirt, and a simple jacket— while many individuals with a mere fraction of his net worth sat in the front row, dripping with $150,000 pieces of jewelry and driving $300,000 vehicles.

Here's the difference between a getting-paid approach and a wealth-building approach to life. Tony paid his NBA players million-dollar salaries with what I could call his petty cash. They looked the part of success, but Tony Ressler exemplified it. While Tony was not dressed what you and I might call "fancy," when you saw him you just knew he was a boss of something. Tony was important, but you didn't know the what, where, and why of it. It was what is in Tony—not on him—that defines the winning state of mind.

Consider the Latinxs and blacks who sell goods—oranges, soft drinks, chips, and mixed fruit—at Crenshaw Boulevard near the on-ramp for the Interstate 10 freeway in Los Angeles where I grew up. These enterprises are the beginning of a store or a business, no different than a Walmart or a Whole Foods. The difference is the mentality of the seller. Marcus Goldman and Samuel Sachs were at one time just two guys selling financial services door to door, but they had a vision. This "aspirational crack" is what separates the ownership class—the winning class—from the rest of us.

Consider winners: public servants like Abraham Lincoln to freedom fighters like Harriett Tubman, freedmen like Frederick Douglass, industrialists like John D. Rockefeller and Andrew Carnegie, inventors like Thomas Edison and Nikola Tesla, leaders of social justice like Dr. King and Andrew Young, real estate developers like Herman J. Russell of Atlanta, automobile magnates like Henry Ford, retailers like Sam Walton, technologists like Bill Gates and Steve Jobs, and entertainers and brand-makers like Quincy Jones, Oprah Winfrey, and Jay-Z.

These winners all have one thing in common: they convinced themselves not only that they could win, but that they were in fact already winners. And that belief is, literally, half the battle.

The destruction of this fundamental belief system, the belief people need to have in themselves, explains almost totally the journey of aspirational frustration shared by at least three distinct groups in America over the past four hundred years. These are the people whose spirit we broke.

You'll read more about these people in the next chapter. But before I come to them, let me finish this important lesson on the importance of believing, the importance of knowing that you not only can win but that in fact you are preprogrammed by God to be a winner. Let me tell you a short and very powerful story.

I went to breakfast with a new friend named Mike Maples Jr. in December of 2019. Mike is a legend in Silicon Valley venture capital investing. He told me about what he described as his "casual" normal family growing up.

Mike described his father as someone who "worked with Bill Gates and Microsoft on software." The way Mike explained it to me, I just presumed that his father was a corporate vice president somewhere within the company. But as Mike continued, unpacking the story and answering my probing questions, it became clear that his dad was a very big deal at Microsoft, right alongside Bill Gates. It turns out his dad was number three in the entire company.

Other than Mike's striking humility in describing his dad's prominence in tech, nothing was particularly jarring about this story—yet. And then Mike told me about when he got started.

Mike was fifteen years old when he started his first business building and selling video games. Fifteen! Now, a kid starting a video game company at fifteen should be enough to qualify as a big deal, but that is nowhere near the moral of the story, nor the shocker. To everyone who thinks they understand what winning really looks like, here's some more information.

At some point in that first year, Mike tells his father that maybe he can sell his video game company to Disney. He was still fifteen. I thought this was audacious thinking for even a forty-five-year-old man like myself, let alone a fifteen-year-old kid. But Mike's dad wasn't impressed like I was. Mike's dad was disappointed. Very disappointed.

Mike's dad said something to young Mike that just blew me away. It also changed his life forever.

"Mike, you have the wrong attitude," he said. "You should be asking yourself, can you *buy* Disney."

Let that sink in for a minute. Reread the above quote. Read it again slowly, and out loud, for those in the back of the room wherever you are.

The senior Mike Maples's view of the world was you should always have a leadership agenda in your life, and that any life strategy you have should be to lead. He was trying to teach his son the same lesson that civil rights leader Dr. Benjamin Mays liked to preach:

"Not failure, but low aim is [the] sin."[1]

Talk about a winning attitude. Talk about being totally underwhelmed with a simple thriving mentality, and having no use at all for a mere surviving mentality.

Mike Jr. is the descendant of that winning home culture. No wonder he is the raging success he is today. From the age of a young child, he was literally coded to win.

Now you might be saying, Of course Mike Jr. is a winner. He grew up with every privilege that means something in America: white, rich, male, and well connected.

So now let me underscore how race, at least, is secondary in this narrative. Let's look at how famed Atlanta-based African American real estate developer Herman Russell business-raised and mentored his granddaughter Mori Russell. Attending Spelman College in Atlanta, Mori had natural leadership and sales skills and the confidence that comes from the Russell family cultural DNA.

At eighteen, Mori decided to launch a jewelry sales business. Her first sales event was a major success, but when she went to brag to her grandfather, Herman Russell gave her anything but unedited praise.

Mr. Russell asked, "How do you count this as a success? You had the event at our restaurant, you used our network of friends, and we paid for the top-flight hors d'oeuvres and drinks. Of course people bought everything you had. You now have to prove that you can do it next time, on your own, anywhere, anytime, and without a lot of expensive assistance."

Mori didn't see this as criticism; for her it was a leadership lesson. And today, she works in a management role in several of the Russell family businesses in Atlanta. She hustles every day and takes nothing for granted. She wakes up every day hungry for a win. Her family has a winning attitude hard-coded into their cultural DNA. They may fall down, but for them, getting back up quickly is the value proposition—because that's what winners do.

Winning is not born, but it is embedded. That's the power of what I call cultural DNA.

My wife, Chaitra, is filled with self-confidence and self-love. So much confidence and love were poured into her life growing up that she is now fearless.

She grew up in a small town of 5,000 called Grafton in West Virginia, and later in an even smaller town of 2,500 called Dillsburg in Pennsylvania. In both places, Chaitra was surrounded by the love of family and the love and safety of small-town friends. In Grafton, her entire street was made up of family members, all of whom showered her with love, confidence, and unconditional support. All that love worked to make her the winner she is today.

When you meet Chaitra today, you meet a smile that begins on the inside and radiates out, connecting you with someone who is obviously also super sharp. Chaitra was one of two black girls in her high school in Dillsburg, but somehow became Homecoming Queen. She was one of the only African Americans and the most popular girl in school.

Mrs. Dalton, Chaitra's mother, was a member of the city council in Grafton—in fact, in 1977 she was the first black member of the council in the city's history. Even so, her greatest success was raising and pouring love and attention into her brilliant twins, Sean and Chaitra—just like my mother did to me. Everyone calls Chaitra's dad "Dr. Dalton," including me. But when he was coming up in Grafton, he didn't get much respect. He struggled in a very poor family, and a football scholarship was his way out. When he came back to Grafton with a bachelor's degree in pharmacy, he tried to get a job at the local pharmacy store. He thought that his competency would be enough, but he was turned down. Dr.

Dalton is absolutely convinced that he was turned away simply because of the color of his skin. From that day forward, he decided that he would never be denied any opportunity in life. He mentally reconditioned himself to win.

A decade later, Dr. Dalton found himself one of three most senior executives at Rite Aid, responsible for expansion and new location selections. His next location selection just happened to be next door to the local pharmacy that had denied him his first simple opportunity. He put them out of business. Now here's the love part. Recently, Dr. Dalton told me he actually felt bad they had to close down.

He told me that he admired that the pharmacy owners were able to work hard and build wealth, put their kids through college, take care of their family, and meet their responsibilities. He said that whatever bias they had against him—and, perhaps, against other black people—was probably just lack of exposure and basic ignorance. Dr. Dalton held no animus or bad feelings for any of them. He was wholly focused on living his best life.

Dr. Dalton went on to buy and sell several businesses, and today he runs the twenty-second-largest black-owned business in America, with more than $200 million in annual revenue. Still a humble and low-key man, he attributes his success to having the right mindset. The reason Dr. Dalton is a winner is because he does not let anything get in his way.

These are the mother and father of my wife, Chaitra, so you can imagine the kind of winning spirit that has been poured into her. The only problem with Chaitra today: she has no fear.

At eighteen years old, she had the confidence and self-belief (chutzpah, or "hootspa" as they say where I grew up) to claim ownership of the URL americanexpress.com. And... it worked! She actually owned that invaluable piece of digital real estate at age eighteen. The only problem is that the Dalton family was friends with the American Express company leadership, and Chaitra was encouraged to just hand it over. I would not have but, as I have already made clear, Chaitra is much nicer than I am.

Chaitra is a love-centric leader and her brilliance, her out-of-the-box thinking, and her absolute inner confidence is no accident. At twenty-two years of age, Chaitra got an offer that took enormous confidence to accept. She was asked to go to China to manage manufacturing for the Donna Karan brands throughout the entire country. She had never lived outside the United States, had never been to Asia, let alone China, and she spoke no Mandarin. But none of this even crossed Chaitra's mind as a barrier.

She went, she worked, and she conquered. She was so good her employer wanted to renew her contract. Chaitra chose not to (she has challenges eating Chinese food to this very day) because she'd met another designer there who made her an offer she could not refuse. It spoke to one of her real passions—fashion *design*, as opposed to manufacture—and before she knew it she was on a team helping to design the 1992 Olympic basketball team jerseys. Confidence and self-esteem through the roof.

Chaitra has known she was a winner from her very first breath in the Dalton household. It was in her cultural DNA.

As for me, I had some clues in my youth, and then one big life lesson from Harvey Baskin sealed my belief in myself as a winner.

As a teenager I decided to take a job as a bus boy in a restaurant—but not just any restaurant. If I was going to work in a restaurant, it was going to be one where I could learn and earn. I decided that it was worth my traveling by bus and car from deep in South-Central Los Angeles to Gladstones for Fish in Pacific Palisades, California, just below Malibu.

At first it was cool. Gladstones's clientele was awesome if your ambition was to be the top local CPA or the top local banker, as this was whom you found yourself serving. But I wanted more. And so I applied for and was hired to be a waiter at arguably the most high-end restaurant in Malibu proper, Geoffrey's Malibu, owned by businessmen and partners Geoffrey Etienne and Harvey Baskin.

As a waiter on the worst night shift of the week (Monday), I got to know both Geoffrey and Harvey within a short time. Soon I was working as their part-time personal assistant during the day and a mediocre waiter by night. In time, the wait job fell away and I took on a full-time post with Harvey Baskin, working out of his exquisite Malibu mansion on the beach. This is where I began to learn the "both" power of relationship capital: when people both like and respect you, they want to do business with you. That's when the big business actually gets done.

Sitting at the hem of Harvey's "Jesus robe" (his daily business uniform was a one-piece cloth robe shirt and open-toed sandals), I got the equivalent of two or three business degrees. Unfortunately, his rise and accomplishments were pre-internet, so most have heard little about his brand of success. I am glad to share through this book this amazing man's name.

But back then, I had no idea what I was experiencing right in front of me. I only saw, as is the problem with youth, all that I was not getting in that job with Harvey. He paid me crap and challenged me often. But he also let me close often enough to see how the business sausage was made, so to speak. He showed me the real art of the deal, but I didn't appreciate it much. And so, having earned little legitimate reason to do so, I pushed, as young people often do. To Harvey's credit, he responded to my pushing by folding me under his supportive arms and nurturing the potential he saw within me.

One day I asked Harvey to dinner. I was focused on the benefit I planned to extract from my friend and boss. I wanted to know how he did it all and how I could do it too.

Harvey chose one of the fanciest restaurants in Venice, California. When the bill came, I pushed the expensive tab to him to pay. He pushed that bill back toward me. Harvey had decided it was time for a lesson, time for me to decide whether I was going to be a winner or whether I was going to become emotional and angry about how unfair the world is (which, by the way, no one wants to hear).

And so, Harvey Baskin leaned in to me and shared a lesson for life that I will remember for the rest of my life. He said, "John, you have to make some decisions. You have to decide, right now, whether you want to pick my brain, or pick my pocket. One lasts longer."

Did I want to "get paid," or did I want to start investing in my true wealth-building capacity? Well, the light came on, my mouth shut up, I paid the bill, and I received the first of what would become a series of vitally important mental software upgrades on how to live life at the tip of the spear.

The winning mentality of Chaitra, Dr. Dalton, Mike Maples Jr. and Sr., and every other big name I've mentioned in this chapter is what drives bold men and women of every race to transform the world as we know it.

Whether it was in their cultural DNA or they figured it out on their own somewhere along the way, they learned how to speak the language of aspirations, capital, and success. They got the memo.

But there are so many more—and growing—in this world who never got that memo. And it's biting the winners and thrivers in the ass.

CHAPTER 3

The Survivors—What's Getting in Their (and Everybody's) Way

The surviving mindset. Defined by a lack of hope and reluctant participation in a system that doesn't seem to work for you. You're just barely getting by. It may not be your fault that you ended up here, but it's critically important that you climb out of this space as soon as is humanly possible. Why?

A surviving mindset is hard to manage around. It needs to be wholly abandoned because, left untreated, you begin to feel empty and unseen, which leads to anger, resentment, and depression. Anger is not a business plan. Being upset, rightly or wrongly, doesn't pay a single bill. Then there's depression. When you undergo a traumatic experience, there's a chance it will define every step you take from that point forward. Your life can become emotional. You may begin reacting instead of responding. Your life choices might start to look more like "ready, fire, aim" than "ready, aim, fire." One of the cruelest realities of those who struggle at the bottom of the economic ladder are the emotional, intellectual, and aspirational scars they're unsuccessfully attempting to leave behind.

Survivors have a state of mind that is more convinced about what cannot happen, than what can. They are experts at what is not possible, at what they are against. They have come to believe, for good reason, that the entire system is against them. And then, quite naturally, what results is an all-too-obvious chip on their shoulder. That little bit of negative vibe is ever present, even if unarticulated with words— and it's a relationship-building killer.

A hallmark of this mentality is being perpetually angry and upset at society and life. But righteous or not, being upset and angry does not "spend," as I like to say. There sure is a lot out there to be angry about but, respectfully, feelings don't pay bills.

Today there is a burgeoning, fast-growing population of people in the surviving-mentality class who are depressed, frustrated, and vexed by America's broken aspirational ladder. Adding to the problem, there is a stalled middle-class "thriving"-mentality group who feel like they are doing nothing more than treading the economic waters in America today. Finally, we have an embarrassingly small group of very privileged and fortunate individuals in the winning-mentality class.

When I was seven years old, I had my first experience with an otherwise wonderful human being who was, unknowingly to me, living 100 percent in survival mode with a survivor mindset. As a result, this man whom I called my uncle

(I learned later he wasn't really related to me, but it didn't matter), had an obsession with finding ways to "get paid" in his life. He saved my life when I was seven. I had fallen backward, hit my head on his porch, and was swallowing my tongue. This man took action, pulled my tongue from my air passage, and literally saved my life. I only wish I could thank him to this very day.

He was a great man, but his survivor mentality was his downfall. After finishing his normal job for the day, he would ride his bike somewhere far away from the neighborhood for a few hours. One day, on his way back from wherever he'd been, a truck followed him and—right in front of me—ran my uncle down, dragging him down the street, mangled bike included, until he was dead. I can recall this traumatic incident in my mind's eye as if it were yesterday. I found out later that my uncle had been selling marijuana in a neighboring community where there was a turf war among gangs.

The Problem with Just "Getting Paid"

My uncle was so desperate to make some money—to "get paid" as they say in Compton, California, where I come from—that he simply wasn't paying attention to the details of his life and his environment, and definitely not to the obvious danger signals around him.

When people are in survival mode they are also highly emotional. They react when they should be responding. And you should never make a serious decision, especially a financial one, when you are emotional. My uncle did that, and he paid the ultimate price of his life.

So many of my friends, then and now, are just as obsessed with making some money—or "finding some paper," as they used to say where I grew up—that they often forget that the *how* is as important as the *what*. If you get the *how* wrong, you may not live long enough to enjoy the *what*. It might just get you killed, especially if you're barely surviving to begin with.

I learned early on that making money was transactional, and pretty easy to do in the short term. A drug dealer can make money. A gang banger or a mobster can make money. A fraudster can make money. The problem is that these jobs can also get you killed. *And* they don't move you out of survivor mode. It was a big a-ha moment in my life when I realized the difference between making money and building wealth. Making money is an activity, a transaction. Building wealth is a mindset—a winner's mindset. More on that later.

When I was nine years old, I had another traumatic experience that intersected with money and the pursuit of it. My best friend at the time was an eighteen-year old named George. He lived down the street from me in Compton, California. He was a straight-A student, and I was a C+ student. I wanted to be like George, but George really didn't know who he wanted to be.

Like so many young people in underserved neighborhoods like the one I grew up in, George was super smart—possibly even brilliant in his potential—but completely lost as an individual. These kids don't know who they are (so often, Dad isn't around for guidance and discipline, and Mom is trying to make enough money to survive), so they emulate whatever they perceive to be "cool" and accepted—no matter how dumb, dead-ended, and dangerous that choice might actually be. Looking back now, this perfectly described my friend George.

I wanted to hang with George, but George wanted to hang around the local gangsters because they had access to fast women and quick money—neither of which last, by the way, but don't mind me being rational here. If poverty were rational, poor people would not be poor. Unfortunate but true. Good people, bad mindset.

George was murdered on a street corner right next to my gangster, next-door neighbor Tweet. By that time I had witnessed or personally experienced close-up three deaths: the death of my parent's marriage and our family unit by age 5, and the murders of two people whom I loved and held dear by age 9. The one thread weaving itself through all three experiences was money.

It was all very clarifying for me. I decided I had had enough of this nonsense. At nine, I wanted to find a better way forward, a more authentic, transparent, and sustainable way to live my life. I wanted to find a way to win.

A Brief History of Survivors in America

It's now time to set an important record straight. Let's make it perfectly clear who makes up America, and how they got here. Not only that, let's discuss which tools they were equipped with and, equally important, which tools they were unjustly denied. And let me preface this discussion by stating emphatically that the groups that were unjustly denied—African Americans, Native Americans, and poor whites—are not somehow inferior in their talents or aspirational reach. They were systematically left out. If anything proves that the real color is green, it is this fact.

As I've mentioned, America is primarily made up of type-A personality dreamers and the descendants of those dreamers. These dreamers came to Ellis Island with little money in their pockets and almost nonexistent relationship capital tied to the powerful and the monied—but they were armed with an unquenchable thirst for achievement and success. They were on an epic quest for their own God-given opportunity. They came from everywhere around the globe to America because they were attracted to her unique idea of freedom.

They came from Europe.

They came from South America.

They came from the Middle East and Asia and India.

They came from Africa.

They came from all over the world, men and women and children alike, armed with a bold dream and unlimited energy and work ethic to get there. Most of all, they came with spirit. A passionate spirit and a belief in their ability to win if simply given the chance.

And so, it makes sense to look at Europe, and see the vast majority of Europeans who are, well, still there. And the vast majority of Asians are still living and working and striving in Asian countries. And the vast majority of Africans and Latin Americans, and those from the Middle East and elsewhere, are still living in their places of origin too. It is completely normal is what I am saying here. Most of them didn't have that obsession with their own expression of freedom, combined with a winning drive and an insatiable appetite for their own brand of success on their own terms. And so, they stayed where they were. All good. Needed, even, for balance and stability in the world.

Most people in the world didn't immigrate to America. But those who did, who came to America of their own will, did so because they were overachieving dreamers—or, as the late civil rights leader Dr. Dorothy I. Height once said about me, "dreamers with shovels in their hands."

I am alluding to the fact that not every American in this great country came here of their own will and because of their dream of freedom and opportunity. There are three very distinct groups—groups of the most amazing and resilient people—who have a different story and who have been treated very differently. They have been unjustly treated by any measure of the human condition, which is a 100 percent understatement of the facts.

They didn't come here to fulfill their dreams. Instead, they came here—or were already here—and had their dreams steamrolled. Their self-esteem and their necessary spirit for self-determination was systematically destroyed. No one taught them how to be industrious and to seek and operationalize self-determination and wealth creation. They were 100 percent in survival mode.

That group of three includes:

- ► African American slaves

- ► Native Americans

- ► Poor whites

African Americans and poor whites didn't come to America because they had a burning desire to win. They either came here by force (in the case of African Americans) or desperation (in the case of poor whites), or they were pushed out of their own native homeland (in the case of Native Americans). For all these groups, America was not the land of freedom and opportunity; it was hell.

More than two-hundred-plus immigrant groups in America *did* largely succeed in living their American Dream. Here is a brief narrative on the three that got tripped up by no fault of their own, as well as the colossal challenges to "coming up" that they have in common.

African Americans were enslaved on American soil. Native Americans were denied their own place and space on American soil. And many of the earliest poor whites were shipped here from Britain as indentured servants, and pretty much "scheduled" to eke out a life of subsistence poverty on American soil. All three groups were in different ways and on differing levels robbed of their dignity, stripped of their spirit, and systematically denied their seat at the table of American opportunity.

No one taught these groups how to be industrious, how to move from survival to thriving to winning. They did not get what I refer to in my last book as "the memo."[1] They were denied the fundamental building blocks that would have allowed them to transition out of "survival mode."

No one is telling the children in these groups that they can work someplace meaningful, let alone start a business at fifteen—let alone dream about purchasing one of the largest businesses in the world at fifteen. Whether any of these children, including Mike Jr., can purchase a company the size of Disney is irrelevant, really. They are never going to win if they don't *believe* that they can—or if they have no one around them who believes they can. And that's how survivors stay down, or at least one of the ways.

And both to underscore the power of belief, or the lack thereof, and to likewise underscore how race and racism—as horrible and disabling as it is in the American success narrative—are not the universal explanation for all that wrongs us, I present to you the December 2017 study by the Federal Reserve Bank of Boston. The results will leave your jaw on the floor.

Researchers used data collected from households in Boston, Miami, Tulsa, Los Angeles, and Washington, DC. In Boston, the research focused on multigenerational African Americans (US blacks), Caribbean blacks (including Haitians), and whites. The results were stunning. The household median net worth for whites was found to be $247,500, the net worth for Caribbean blacks was $12,000, and for US blacks, $8. The average net worth of US blacks was $8. And as the headline of *The Boston Globe* said at the time, "That was no typo."[2]

Now, all of these numbers are troubling, to say the least,

but one data point just jumps out at me and makes one thing patently clear. If being black was the total and complete problem in America, then either all black people in the United States—whether they were multigenerational African American, blacks from the Caribbean, or dark people from elsewhere—should have the distressing net worth of $12,000, or the devastatingly bad one of $8. It should be one or the other—at least it should be close. And so, the unfair head start given to white America set aside, something else is going on here, and I believe it is tied to belief, to mindset. I think it has to do with whether different groups are saddled with a survivors' mentality, a thriving mentality, or whether they were lucky enough to claim a winning mentality.

Success by the Numbers

At the opening of *The Black Godfather,* which chronicles the incredible life story of entertainment mogul Clarence Avant, you hear Clarence saying in a powerful voice:

> "Life is about one thing: numbers.... [It] begins with a number and ends with a number.... Nothing else."[3]

This is more true than we know.

The first number is of course your birth date. That's a number. And then you have your maturity date when you pass on to glory, hopefully. That's a number also. The question, then, is not when you are born or how many years you live, but what you do with the time that you have. Life is all in the how, not so much the what.

We don't know how long we are going to live, but we absolutely know that one day we will die, so why are we always surprised? We should be focused on the footprints we leave in the sands of time, while we are here. What is our contribution? What is our legacy?

Here are the numbers that really matter in life:

If I get just a high school education, versus a college education, how much money will I be leaving on the table at the end of my working life?

If I work to live, and my partner works to invest (using their income to build wealth for the family), how much more will our family be worth? How much wealth will we create this way, versus one or both of us simply living in the moment, living just to pay current bills?

Do people with higher net worth get better treatment and customer service? Do they get shortcuts to the front of the line, such as the red carpet lane for airplane boarding, or the assignment of their own private banker?

Am I considering the income and wealth-building ability of someone before I make a marriage decision? Am I considering my mate's credit score as I sort out the current aspirational mentality of the one I plan to build a life with? In addition to marrying for love, am I also marrying for the financial sharing and the safety and financial security, as well as the economic protections that marriage affords our future children?

Is the number-one cause for divorce a number? Yes, it's called zero. Broke. No dinero. The number-one cause for divorce is money, not infidelity or "we just don't get along anymore." It's a lot easier to get along with someone who has six or more zeros associated with their bank balance than with someone with less.

If I have nine broke people around me, what are the chances that I will be the tenth? (High, I might add. We model what we see.)

What about zip code? Your zip code is more predictive of your chance for success than your racial makeup or your political party.

Going even deeper, what is the average credit score of the people within my zip code? This number is an absolute predictor of the aspirational environment—or, conversely, the imminent danger—associated with your community culture. That number defines your community DNA.

Let's talk a bit more about community and cultural DNA and how it factors into your ability to survive, thrive, or win.

Everyone seems to know the story of Steve Jobs, the genius cofounder of Apple, Inc. But precious few understand or appreciate the back story.

Mr. Jobs was the result of a love interest between a mainstream (Caucasian) woman and a Jordanian man. The father of the young lady wouldn't stand for the match and demanded that the child be put up for adoption. The criteria set for that adoption was that the family be wealthy with an impeccable pedigree and background. They found a good family, but then the adoption fell through. Though the second applicants weren't what they had in mind, they accepted the adoption anyway. That "backup" family, the Jobs family, was middle-class with a father who was an engineer in the San Francisco Bay Area.

Steve ended up living in the heart of Silicon Valley, around the corner from a young man by the name of Steve Wozniak. Wozniak was a young engineering phenom; Jobs honed his genius for design, strategy, marketing, and sales. The two collected a few other young dreamers and believers with a winning mentality from the neighborhood and, ultimately, a couple of investors they knew in and around the area. With the Jobs's family garage as their first office, Apple was born. Now, the founding story of Apple is, of course, much more complicated and involved than this, but the lesson remains the same no matter how you tell it:

The zip code, the cultural DNA, and the credit score (read: the hope and upwardly mobile aspiration and access to credit and capital) in Silicon Valley ensured that the dream of Apple became a reality.

Let me flip the script, so you can see clearly how much the people around you matter to your up-from-nothing story.

Let's now take Steve Jobs, the son of a Middle Eastern, Jordanian immigrant, and instead have him adopted by a low-wealth family led by a single mother in Detroit or on the south side of Chicago. With crime and gunshots surrounding his home, and a 500-credit-score environment, what happens to that kid? Same kid. Same brilliance.

This version of Steve Jobs probably does not found Apple, one of the wealthiest companies in the world. This version of Steve Jobs takes his same genius and ability to strategize, market, and sell to become the biggest drug dealer the city has ever seen. The result of this path is that this version of Steve Jobs is either shot and killed or locked up after a ten-year run. Story over.

When Survivors Can't Thrive, We All Lose

The problem with the growing number of people in America who feel like they're just surviving, who are spiritually and economically depressed, is that it messes with *all* of our business plans.

What are the survivors turning to in order to survive? "Getting paid" jobs like dealing drugs. Numbing their depression through abuse of alcohol and other substances. Taking out their (justifiable) anger at the world on their loved ones with physical and emotional violence. Voting against their best interests because they can't see past the short-term mentality of somehow making it through the day.

Think of the lost potential and productivity of these intelligent, hard-working groups who are so burdened by surviving that they can't even begin to process how to break out of this mental cage. Think about the economic leakage of potential in, to, and for America, or anywhere else for that matter. What would happen if these groups, who together number one hundred million, became GDP creators instead?

We, every one of us in America, cannot afford to have these groups not contributing. They are dragging down the index through no fault of their own. They are dragging us all down. And by not supporting them, not giving them a hand in coming up, *we* are helping to drag all of *us* down.

The problem is we are not working together to help the survivors come up. Instead, the thrivers and winners are creating private communities so they don't have to deal with the turmoil the survivors are unintentionally creating. Instead, we are becoming increasingly polarized because we don't want to deal with "other people's problems." What we are not realizing is that other people's problems are our problems and they are America's problems. And if we don't solve them, we will all lose. America will lose. (Some would say America is already losing, but I don't believe that.)

A house divided will not stand. That's biblical. The thrivers and winners cannot insulate themselves from the impending explosion of survivors' desperation. And that is why I say this book is selfish—and it's about our collective uplift.

Let us lift up the depressed and broken-spirited because when these people are winning then America wins. Because if my rich friends want to stay rich, then my poor friends have to do better—or, in truth, then somebody has to help my poor friends do better.

What America needs to produce once again, at scale, are true ladder-climbers from the surviving class to the thriving class and the thriving class to the winning class (which includes all of us). This means fixing that doggone aspirational ladder I keep talking about over and over and over again. What we need is a country of winners.

If I were China or Russia, I could come up with no more

brilliant plan to unseat America—as the sole superpower in the world, the largest economy in the world, and the undisputed champion of freedom and democracy for all in the world—than to divide her. Than to convince her citizens that a group or groups within America are their enemy, that the real problem lies somewhere in their own states, in their own cities, in their own communities, or even on their own blocks. To give us reasons to stop believing in ourselves, yet alone in each other. To believe that we cannot work together, to sow the seeds of distrust among us, making us think that we are not brothers and sisters and friends all on the same team. To make us expend useless, totally nonproductive energy fighting and arguing with each other, talking past each other, graduating to indifference toward each other and, ultimately, to radical indifference toward each other.

It is possible that the world is already at war, without bombs and bullets—an economic war, as my friend Jim Clifton, CEO of Gallup, said in his brilliant book *The Coming Jobs War*. And the best way to unseat America from that economic throne is to strip her of her primary asset: the optimistic, striving, aspirational, hopeful, unified will of her people.

But in this book I am not attempting to save America from the Russians or the Chinese—though both countries are without question after what we've got. I am attempting to save us from ourselves.

These two countries have taken countless pages out of our success story rule book over the decades, but now they see and sense a little blood in the water and they want more.

This "blood in the water" is our dissension, our divisions among ourselves. It is our doesn't-make-much-sense-but-it's-still-the-case "dislike" we Americans often possess for one another.

We are arguing over stupid stuff like what color other people are, or where they came from, or which church they go to, or who they go with, and what gender that person is, and so on and on. Even the more weighty stuff we argue about, like how we can fix the wrongs of our past, are beside the point; they don't move us forward. Here we are finding not-very-creative or unique ways to dislike and disrespect and argue with one another. And not only are Russia and China eating it all up—we're shooting ourselves in the collective foot.

CHAPTER 4

The Five Pillars of Success

I have taken pains to acknowledge that racism still very much exists in this country today. I'll say it again racism is real. Very real. But race and racism alone cannot explain the general failure to rise of certain disadvantaged groups, one of whom is poor whites.

Racism negatively affected my African American mother and father, and their parents, and their parents' parents. My great-grandparents, and possibly my grandparents, as children were slaves in the American South, brutalized by a system that illegally yet systematically transferred the wealth of their God-given initiative to others.

But as brutal and unfair as racism was and is, ultimately, it did not hold back the broad cross-section of my family. That's because we got something right, even if accidentally so. My family used a makeshift formula for success in America almost in spite of required support, not because of it.

Likewise, consider the inspiring modern-immigrant tales of my hard-working African brothers and sisters who came to America on their own energy. And the enterprising stories of my Caribbean brothers and sisters who came from a whole range of island nations to America of their own volition. They also got right something really important, something that allowed them to rise up from nothing in spite of the very real limitations tied to race and racism.

You can also look at my Jewish brothers and sisters, who had to deal with the horrors of the Holocaust and a very targeted campaign to exterminate their race, the result of which was the systematic murder of fully one-third of their people worldwide at the time—six million. Despite the audacity of the discrimination they faced, they as a group have also managed to rise up. Today, of about fifteen million Jews worldwide, approximately half live in the United States. This group of oppressed people clearly figured out a couple of things.

In this section, I am going to unpack what distinguished the two-hundred-plus mostly mainstream ethnic groups—including Jews, Caribbean blacks, and modern African immigrants—who immigrated to America and made it a superpower. I will also break down what has been missing for the three groups who have not—collectively—come up from nothing: African Americans, Native Americans, and poor whites originally from Great Britain.

Now, of course, not all African Americans, Native Americans, and poor whites in America have failed. In fact, there are countless inspiring stories of the *exact opposite* being true—stories of proud, accomplished, and highly successful

African Americans and others becoming immensely successful. Against all odds, they achieved success. But this is not a book about the outliers.

I am explicitly *not* talking here about exceptions to any rule. I am talking about *the* rule, the same rule that allowed, in fact facilitated, the mainstream success of the majority of ethnic groups in America as they flowed from wherever, flowing mostly through the freedom port of Ellis Island.

Could there be a set of rules, similar to a standardized math formula, that lays out a framework for why certain groups might succeed in America? Could this framework also explain why other groups—of equal if not greater "merit"—might fail, despite hard work, smarts, and their best efforts?

I believe there is. And only once the pillars of this framework for success are available to all Americans equally can we fulfill our collective dream of winning.

The five pillars of success are:

► Massive Education

► Understanding the Numbers

► Family Structure and Resiliency

► Self-Esteem and Confidence

► Role Models

Let's unpack them. I'll use my own story to show you that anybody, no matter where they come from, if they have access to these five pillars can come up from nothing. I was lucky. I was an exception to the rule. Let's make access to these pillars the rule.

Education

When the world seems to be stacked against you, the great-est leveler of inequality, opportunity, and confidence is edu-cation—and consuming and absorbing as much education as you can possibly handle. As much education as you could possibly jam down your throat, to paraphrase former US president Lyndon Baines Johnson.

Education is and always has been the great emancipator, no matter your station or background in life. When you know better, you do better. And once you get an education, no one can repossess it. It is yours for life.

Your life is expanded and deepened—and better—because of the education you feed your inner soul.

I did not graduate from college, but I no doubt got a higher education. I chose a different approach to success in my early years: leaving high school early to pursue opportunities in business and entrepreneurship (obtaining a GED degree, which Chris Rock calls a "Good Enough Diploma"), and later leaving college to do the same.

That said, I never stopped learning. If anything, I became even more obsessed with obtaining what I consider a world-class higher education.

As for the tools of learning, I love books in particular, because I can always tuck a favorite in my briefcase or a few in my travel bag. For as long as I can remember, I have had home offices with every wall filled with books. Years ago I remember heading to Maui for my annual retreat, checking at the airport a large duffle bag filled with nothing but books

I planned to read while there. (Thank God we're in the digital age now.)

I also learned to ask a *lot* of questions of highly successful people. I once asked my friend, brother, and mentor, the iconic Quincy Jones, "How did you get so smart?" He told me, "John, I'm just nosy as hell. I want to know everything, about everything." I followed Q's lead.

Every person I've met in my life equated to someone I could help or someone who might help me—as an employee or collaborator, or someone I could sell my vision to, or someone who could make me smarter (a mentor), or someone who might invest with me, or someone who might partner with me. Literally everyone I met represented opportunity. Everyone had a purpose. Because everyone *has* a purpose.

The education that mattered the most, perhaps, was in how the world really works. The math. The money. That capitalism thing. The fact that, on some level, we are each a capitalist. We are using our own human capital, our talents, our skills, to generate "a return on our invested time and energy" (revenue, paycheck, etcetera) and using "the proceeds" to live, and to take care of our lives, family, and responsibilities. I received an education on the numbers. More on that in the next section.

The Numbers

While not understanding how money, economics, and the numbers work is a real problem for everyone today, it was an absolute death-nell crisis situation for former slaves back in 1865. That was why in March of 1865 President Abraham Lincoln created a bank to teach freed slaves about money: the Freedman's Bank. Sadly, Lincoln was murdered the following month, and the bank's future was thrown into jeopardy.

The bank was so important to the lifeblood of the newly emancipated African American population that none other than abolitionist and social reformer Frederick Douglass tried to save it. Frederick Douglass even invested $10,000 of his own money to save the bank (something akin to $20 million today), but with the new institution's organizational protector gone, there was no hope. As a result, African Americans just never got "the memo" on free enterprise, capitalism, business, entrepreneurship, ownership, and opportunity. They were never exposed to the winning, wealth-building mindset that is critical to succeeding in a free enterprise democracy such as America.

Fortunately for me, my family made sure that I came out of the womb knowing the numbers to win in America.

My paternal grandfather RB Smith was born in 1871, during the American Reconstruction, right after the legal end of slavery in 1865 (although many Southern areas still engaged in the horrific practice).[1] It is very probable that RB's father and mother were slaves, and also possible that RB himself was born into illegal slavery in 1871. One or both of my great-grandparents were definitely slaves in Mississippi. I had to write this again, just to let it sink in.

By 1940, RB owned a farm. At a time when most African Americans were still trying to regain their most basic sense of their own human dignity, RB was a landowner. According to the 1940 census, the farm was worth $700 at that time. This means that my grandfather was a businessman. Despite all the racial barriers he faced, it was somehow in his DNA to be a stakeholder, to own something.

For fifty-four years my father, Johnnie Will Smith, owned his cement-contracting business. My mother, Juanita Smith, worked a standard hourly wage job at McDonnell Douglas Aircraft and ran two side businesses. A mastery of the numbers was in my parents' DNA, and I was the beneficiary of that knowledge.

My mother knew the numbers for success, but that didn't mean success was easy coming. My mother, her four sisters, and one brother had a hard road growing up in East St. Louis, Illinois. This was the 1940s. Unfortunately, my mother's father died a year or two before Social Security was enacted. The result was that my grandmother found herself alone, solely responsible for six kids, and with zero resource support from the local, state, or federal government.

Back then, the state of Illinois authorities recommended breaking up the family and sending the five girls in two different directions. The assumption was that, if three of the kids could be sent to a family member in Mississippi, then the other girls could stay with their mother in Illinois, and maybe they could receive some level of support. Of course, this would have resulted in the utter destruction of the family unit, not to mention the end of any active, positive mentoring and role-modeling from mother to daughters. I'll talk more on the immeasurable value of role-modeling later.

To her credit, and I will forever be appreciative of this

unselfish act on her part, my grandmother Vesta Murray decided that all of the girls should stay together. But that also meant that each would have to pitch in to survive. The result was alternate levels of emotional pain and financial stress that should never be visited on a girl of any age, let alone my mother, who was about two at the time.

When Mom was a little older, about nine, she made a little money working in rich people's homes. Every time she came back from her job, her mother would ask her, "What did you make today?" And whatever she made went straight out of her pocket to her mother's. But the trouble was, my mother saw that her mother had a problem with gambling, so she decided she needed to do a little mothering of her own. If Mom made fifty cents working (earning twenty-five cents an hour), she would tell her mother she only made twenty-five cents.

She learned the hard way that she had to be a saver—not for a rainy day but possibly for the next day. This habit paid dividends in my mother's life for years, even decades, into the future.

At five years old, I witnessed my mother and father fighting right in front of me. My father had hit my mother, and my sister had placed the phone in my hand as she rang up the police. But at that very moment, my mother flipped the script and struck my dad, and I got confused and I think I hung up the phone. My mom and dad argued about many things, but at the core, their fights were about money: who got it, who spoke to it, and why it was spent.

My mentor, civil rights icon and ambassador Andrew

Young, has always said that men (and women) fail for three reasons: arrogance, pride, and greed. My dad was not greedy, nor was he arrogant, but he was full of pride. And pride goeth before the fall, as they say.

My dad could make the money, but he simply could not keep it. My dad would not ask my mother for help to manage their money, which is a collaborative act to building wealth. My mother was a financial genius both then and now, but my dad simply refused her assistance with the numbers. And, as the Bible says, a house divided cannot stand.

My dad bid jobs for his concrete-masonry business, but because my dad didn't understand the math, because he wasn't financially literate, he made crippling mistakes on his bids. If his competitor bid a job for a concrete driveway installation at $1,200, then my dad, the ever-competitive businessman, would bid $900. The problem is that the $1,200 bid was the more logical bid. My dad bid countless jobs where he ended up spending more on the job than the job was worth. The effect was that the more money he made, the broker we got.

There was also the time we purchased a prime eight-unit apartment building for $18,000 (worth millions today, by the way). We lived in the front unit and could pay the mortgage on that and two units. That left five units available to bring in free cashflow for our living expenses and savings. That was the plan, but unfortunately, that was not how it worked out, because my father was not smart when it came to managing money. We lost the entire investment, including our home. Generational wealth—all lost.

My mother saved $4,000 so she could send my brother to a college of his choice. When my dad took that money, that was it. She'd had it. My father had messed with her business plan one too many times. And that was the beginning of the end of their marriage. It was also the end of generational wealth creation for our family at that time.

Soon thereafter, we'd lost everything, including each other. My mother and the children went in one direction, and my father went in another. The family unit was broken, but the family foundation remained strong, thanks to my mother.

The Magic Bullet Called Profit

My first hands-on lesson about the numbers came when I started my own business at the ripe age of nine (almost ten): the Neighborhood Candy House. All I needed was an investor. I didn't have Warren Buffett's number back then, so I hit up my mother instead. She said no way. I had no experience, she told me, and I had to learn that life offers me no handouts or easy rides. She offered me a $40 short-term loan instead, and a ride to Smart & Final, the place where Mr. Mac, owner of the local liquor store that also sold candy, bought his inventory. I knew because I unpacked the inventory in the back! (More on that later.)

Within an hour of arrival, I had the owners of Smart & Final captivated. They agreed to sell me some candy wholesale, even though I had nothing close to a wholesale license, and they even donated a few candy display racks to my start-up. I will never forget the graciousness they showed me, the way they staked my nine-year-old self. It is little things like this that kids—and adults—remember long after. For me, it reaffirmed, in this critical moment, that I was on the right path. It spun me forward.

My next act was my first business lesson: I ate half of my inventory in a day. To this day I am not overly fond of candy, probably for this reason. I learned that day to not profile, to not be a turkey. I learned to not confuse *business* within *busyness*. Years later this translated into the business lesson: don't buy anything before you can afford it. The formula is very specific: real, sustainable business revenue to pay for the business, profit margin to go to my investors, and then living expenses for me, in that order.

I was able to sell the remaining inventory of candy, and discovered to my surprise that I made enough on half of the original inventory to go back and purchase a whole new inventory for my fledgling business. This lightbulb moment made it perfectly clear to me why capitalism exists and why people of every race, creed, and stripe love it.

But let's talk a little bit more about this magic bullet called profit.

In the adult world, in Mr. Mac's world, "profit over cost of sales" allowed him to pay his mortgage and auto loan and go on an annual vacation. This spent profit then funded some other small business's cost of doing business. This profit allowed him to raise his family and send his children to the college or university of their choice—and to pay his taxes, which in turn paid for community infrastructure and the public good, like public safety, lights and sidewalks, public education, and sanitation.

After a short period of strong sales from my candy shop, headquartered in the den of my mother's home, I effectively put Mr. Mac's liquor store out of the candy business. This was not only a cool thing for my self-esteem and confidence, it was also a public service. No child should have to walk through the aisles of an adult liquor store simply to buy candy. This was the beginning of the "doing good and doing well" ethos in my business life.

No one forced any of my customers to buy my candy. They could have easily walked down the street to my adult competitor. But I was on their route to school, I had better inventory (or at least I thought), and I was priced 10 percent below the same items in Mr. Mac's store. And so they bought my candy, thought it was a great value for them, and kept coming back. This allowed me to expand my offerings and hire my local friends to make a part-time income for themselves—today we call this job creation—and, after the dust settled, I had a nice little profit left over for me. I spent this on girls and then went broke. Yet another lesson learned.

Just like the Operation HOPE client who secures a forty-point increase in their credit score, this early win for a by-then ten-year-old entrepreneur changed my life and outlook on life forever. I was launched and nothing and no one was going to stop me. I knew I was a winner, even before I knew what winning would look like for me.

The Family

A strong family structure means everything, especially at certain times in your life. For me, when I was a small child, it meant everything that my mother told me she loved me every day. Thank you, Ms. Juanita Smith. There is nothing more powerful than a child being told they are loved. I also have to thank my father, Mr. Johnnie Will Smith, who showed me that I could be a businessman by being one himself.

After setting off to drive from California to Detroit, Michigan, to purchase a new car—in and of itself a powerful show of aspirational success—my father, Mr. Johnnie Will Smith, decided to make a brief stop in East St. Louis. He never made it to Detroit.

It was in East St. Louis, one of the poorest cities in America—both then and now—that he met the lady that would change all of our lives forever: my mother, Ms. Juanita Murray. From the moment dad saw my mother, he immediately professed his undying love to her. Within twenty-four hours, he had asked her to marry him.

My mother, back when she was Ms. Juanita Murray, was ambitious enough that she told the admiring Johnnie Smith to move her and her two kids (my older siblings) out of East St. Louis to Southern California, two thousand miles away. If he did, she would agree to marry him. They had only met that week! She asked only for enough time to sell some furniture and pack up her clothes and kids, my brother Dave "Donnie" Harris III and my sister Mara Lamont "Montie"

Hoskins. This was in 1965. I came later, born on February 6, 1966, at Good Samaritan Hospital at seven-something in the morning—*in* Southern California.

These two committed people, with a shared passion for aspiration and uplift for their family and with a thriving mentality, did the near impossible: they worked hard and saved money. They were smart, using my dad's income to live on and my mother's ancillary income for investments and wealth-building.

Once they got to Southern California, my mother got a job at McDonnell Douglas Aircraft (now Boeing). In time, she became a business owner of sorts herself, selling handmade candy and handicrafts to her coworkers on the side so that she could save up enough money for a down payment on her first home. And do you recall what my first business was? The Neighborhood Candy House. As ambassador Andrew Young likes to say, "Coincidence is God's way of staying anonymous."

In their years together, my mom and dad purchased their first home, built a cement-contracting business, built a nursery business, purchased and ran a gas station on the southeast corner of Vernon and Normandie, and purchased the previously mentioned eight-unit apartment building on Santa Barbara Boulevard (later renamed Martin Luther King, Jr. Boulevard). For a time, the Smith family was very successful. And then they hit a wall. My dad not knowing the numbers—and not leaning on my mother's financial genius—led to the failure of our family business plan.

Even so, I was born lucky. I wasn't born brilliant, but I

was lucky and fortunate enough to have Johnnie Will Smith and Juanita Smith as my parents. This changed and formed everything—and I mean everything—in my young life.

When I spoke with top hip-hop star Quavo recently, he confirmed three things I know about him. One, he grew up in a really tough environment. Two, someone in his life regularly told him that they loved him and that he could do anything. And three, he knew from the very start that he was a winner. When you are down and seemingly out, I see these three similarities constantly at work.

Quavo's mother was a lot like my own, meaning she showered me with her love and her confidence in me. But this hadn't been her beginning, nor that of the majority of her siblings.

My mother didn't grow up lucky like me. She and her sister Emma didn't grow up hearing they were loved every day of their lives. They got just the opposite: her mother and stepfather told them they would never amount to anything. She learned to doubt, and question herself and her value, and to wonder, understandably so, why parents would say such a thing to a child.

Their parents did not provide them with the family structure they needed to be winners. But, thankfully, other family members stepped up to provide that structure. Their cousin Aunt Dorothy (don't ask me why they called her "Auntie") encouraged Mom and Emma to stand tall. She told them that they were somebody. Their older brother was also a father figure to them; he helped them to reshape their image of a black man into something positive.

My mother and aunt also had a secret weapon: their faith in God.

When my mother was nine years old, she asked the Lord, "If you allow me to grow up and to have children of my own, I hope I can raise my kids better than I am being raised right now." Later on, at age thirty-six, my mother wrote a letter to the Lord, putting that early prayer into writing. She formally asked for help from a higher power to guide her motherhood experience with and for her children. My mother had decided that she was all in.

You see, my mother knew she was a winner, even at nine years old. She knew that she had a winning streak buried deep inside of her. She decided to talk to the Lord to help unleash that power in herself.

Today, my life plan looks more like a business plan: total nonemotional, focused execution. But the steps my mother took to help me make that happen were the much harder ones. Much harder.

The game-changer in my young life, the thing that convinced me I was somebody, and the thing that got me through, despite all of the challenges, setbacks, and disappointments, was simply this: my mother told me that she loved me, every day of my life. Every day.

I have always known that I was somebody. There were times when I was broke but I have never, ever been poor. Being broke is a temporary economic condition, but being poor is a disabling state of mind, a depressed condition of one's spirit. It's how survivors feel. I decided that I would never, ever be poor. Or, shall I say, my mother decided it for me.

My mother's life plan looked more like direct outtakes from the Bible, and she was totally emotionally and passionately bound up in it. She moved, over time, from youthful pain to adult purpose, from an emotional commitment to living her best life (for her kids at least) to a serious focus on and around love-based achievement. She did not have financial wealth to offer her kids, and she did not have a great support system around her life, so she decided to give us the only things she was in control of and had in massive supply: love, time, and direction. My mother had a business plan to make her children winners, and she was not going to let anyone get in the way of it.

Self-Esteem and Confidence

Self-esteem is how you feel about yourself, the inside you. Confidence is how you express your competence or competencies, the outside you. Both matter.

Quincy Jones once told me, "Not one ounce of my self-esteem depends on someone else's acceptance of me." Over the years, as I was actively ridiculed, with people all around me literally rolling their eyes at my pursuit of my dreams, I took his words to heart.

Early in my business career, certain business types encouraged me to just focus on using my sales skills to "make money" any (legal) way that I could. Even back then, I knew that was a very short-term view of both the world and my potential in the world. They did not see me as I did—as a winner—before I visibly won. And so I didn't take their advice. I did something that most everyone around me ignored, or placed on the back burner—I focused on the inner development of my true and unique self.

I accepted what my new friend Dr. Deepak Chopra said to all of us in his book *The Seven Spiritual Laws of Success:* "We're not human beings that have...spiritual experiences, we're spiritual beings, that have...human experiences."[2] Translation: energy matters. Ever since I reached this realization myself, I focused on finding the positive (path) in most everything around me, in recognizing the value of having positive and productive people around me. People who were and are "about something"—people who loved themselves, or at least tried to, and so would not have a problem sending love and good energy to me too.

I focused on becoming more conscious and aware of what made me and the world around me tick. I focused on getting out of my own way, on my own self-talk, and on my number-one spiritual goal for myself: becoming reasonably comfortable in my own skin. This would become the gift that just keeps on giving.

When I was coming up, I was very tender and sensitive about anything that anyone said about me that was not complimentary. When someone said something "bad" about me, I felt wounded. But today, I find that I am quick to point out my own limitations before anyone else does. But doing that is not some form of self-sabotage or self-hate. It's just the opposite, actually. It is total self-acceptance. Because I realized that no one is perfect, and that there is no perfect, that we are all simply striving to become reasonably comfortable in our own skin. Ideally we can be perfectly imperfect, meaning that we can accept and acknowledge all of ourselves, the good and the bad, as whole and complete.

I hope we can accept that we are not as good as our compliments nor as bad as our critiques—especially those we level against ourselves. I want all of us to simply be happy enough with who we are. Did you know that the greatest compliment you can give yourself is to simply say, "I Am"?

I was teased from childhood through to young adulthood through to—well, until I decided that I'd had enough. And when I decided that it would stop, it wasn't some great big dramatic expression of my feelings. In fact, ultimately, it had very little to do with anyone else.

I didn't have any financial capital. I didn't have a trust fund. I didn't have wealthy parents. I was not passed down a business asset. I didn't belong to the right clubs, whatever that means, nor attend the right schools—so I had to find a way to build for myself. I decided that I was the central asset, but I would not sing, dance, run, bounce or hit a ball (with given respect to all those who have, and do). Those were not my gifts. They were not my talents. I was going to rock a balance sheet. I was going to master building wealth, and companies, and public brands.

I decided it would stop because I had decided that I was enough. I had decided, as I said in my book *Love Leadership*, that my "vulnerability was actually strength. But very few people were tough enough to be soft."

I was going to open new territories, and expand and grow opportunities. I was going to maximize the hidden talents of all who looked like me, of all who came from where I came from. And I was going to prove that you could both do well and do good. I was going to build a brand about that. And I was going to do it at scale. Global was my marketplace target. And so I started with the power of me and I leveraged me.

There is no more important accomplishment in this world than learning to become reasonably comfortable in your own skin. And don't expect everyone—or maybe even anyone early on—to cosign your vision or even your life choices. You have to be comfortable that the real product in your life is you. What you're really selling is you, and you are worth your asking price (and more).

Once you get your mind right, and you've convinced yourself that you can win, you have to then know what your role is: what represents your version of your best self, what brings about your highest levels of self-esteem and confidence. And then you can act and execute with laser precision.

I always knew that I wanted to build something from nothing, to be rich and successful—legally. And I also knew I wanted to help my community. When I looked around as a kid, all I could see was destruction and pain, examples of what I refer to as PPPD—prison, probation, parole, and death—in every direction. I decided that if—no, when—I became successful as an entrepreneur, I was going to do something about the conditions of my neighborhood. And I never questioned my decision; I just wondered what that role was called.

I knew instinctively that I did not desire to be a civil rights leader, nor a grassroots community leader, since that was not my calling. But I wanted to be in a position to help both. I found out that this position in life was called a philanthropist, and so I decided to be that too. And that's what ultimately evolved out of my entrepreneurship: a commitment to, and a resource pool for, community-based philanthropy and community economic empowerment, at scale. That is who I am today.

Once I had decided that I would be an entrepreneur, it was like someone flipped a switch in my brain, turning on the endorphins on the right side, where self-esteem, confidence, creativity, hope, optimism, belief, and dreaming all live. That side of my brain had previously only been transactional in nature and focused on surviving—just as my family and everyone around me was. Everyone around me had a surviving mentality, and so I did as well. Makes perfect sense. We all model what we see. More on that in the next section.

A lot of people invest a great amount of their valuable time doing precisely the wrong job in their life because they don't know—they have not fully recognized—what their gifts are. My dear friend John Bartling, vice chairman of Deutsche Bank, shared with me a brilliantly simple framework for figuring out what your strengths are, where your self-esteem and confidence lie. He talks about the three main roles of the people who contribute to society and how they work together: Hunter, Skinner, and Cook. There's also the Spectator, but that's not a role anyone should aspire to. I'll go over them all here. Figure out which one best represents you.

The Hunter is the one who closes the deal, who makes the sale—the one who is not afraid to make the sale. It is the person who calls one hundred times knowing they will get ninety-eight replies of "no"—but the two "yes" responses they get are all they need to make another one hundred calls. The Hunter brings in the kill, so to speak.

In the classic nuclear family example, the father is the Hunter bringing in the resources that allow for the mother to make the meal and turn the house into a home. But even in this traditional setting the wife can be the Hunter too. A father might be the Hunter in his professional life while the mother is the Hunter at home, like my mother was. She was the one bringing in all the resources to lay down the family values, raise the children, make sound educational decisions, direct contractors on the house build, manage the household budget, and myriad other life-changing decisions that get little to no credit from the outside world.

In my work, I am the Hunter. I know my role, it suits me, and I'm proud of it. But at home, the situation is completely different. With respect to my own quality of life, my wife, Chaitra Dalton Bryant, fills that role. When it comes to saving lives through health and well-being, Chaitra is the focused, on-fire, unrelenting Hunter.

The Skinner is, of course, not a literal interpretation. Think of it as the preparer. The Skinner is the person who takes the food that the Hunter has delivered to the household and uses their expertise to prepare that food, turning it from raw fuel into something suitable for a meal.

In the business environment, the Hunter makes the sale, brings in that new partnership or client or agreement, and the Skinner is the one that ensures that the organization can and will deliver what the Hunter promises. Skinners are the analysts, underwriters, reviewers, data crunchers and researchers, engineers, accountants, and attorneys. This role represents everyone on the inside of the sale.

The Cook is the role easiest to visualize in the household. The Hunter brings in the food, the Skinner prepares the food, and the Cook turns it into a meal. The Hunter may help to purchase a house for the family, but the Cook turns that house into a home.

In a business context, the Cook and the Skinner are just as important as the Hunter in the sales cycle. The Cook is the principal Promise Keeper. For instance, at Operation HOPE, the philanthropic organization that I founded, one of our amazing leaders that plays the role of Hunter is Mrs. Mary Ehrsam, president of HOPE Partnerships. My longtime friend and president of HOPE Programs, Lance Triggs, is the Cook. My long-term chief of staff, Rachael Doff, has always been our chief Skinner. She makes sure that everything in the middle has integrity and works together. All three of these leaders have been with me for more than twenty years each.

There are other amazing leaders within HOPE who play versions or combinations of these roles as well, like our CFO Brian Betts (deputy Hunter, Skinner, and Cook), our head-of-data leader Elaine Hungenberg, and our government leader Jena Roscoe. Most of the members of this crack team—I call them the Special Forces for Community Empowerment and Uplift—can multitask and do multiple roles within the organization, ensuring that at all times Operation HOPE can sell, build, evaluate, and deliver.

And then, unfortunately, there is a bonus role that no serious person should actually want: the role of the Spectator.

The Spectator is particularly fascinating to me because, interestingly enough, this group tends to have the most to say. This group tends to have the biggest, boldest, and most vocal opinions. They spend an outsized amount of time on social media, for instance, talking about other people's lives, and other people's business. But here's the thing: the Spectator gets paid for none of that activity—not even a fee for spiking the social media relevance of the people they're talking about. They own nothing and they produce nothing of worth.

Look at your organization, where you work or lead, and ask yourself: Who plays which role? And now take a peek at your family and assess who is responsible for what's being delivered. People need to figure out their strengths and gain self-esteem and confidence from their roles, whether they are the Hunter, the Skinner, or the Cook. But, again, I discourage anyone from being the Spectator. Spectators are on the sidelines; they don't win anything.

To win in America, to build wealth, to have the freedom of self-determination, we all need to be more than Spectators. Spectators aren't even in the game.

Role Models

I am a businessman today because my father was. I love myself because my mother loved me and told me to love myself. I know I am somebody because I was treated like I was somebody, because I surrounded myself with "somebodys."

One of those "somebodys" was a banker who made several visits to my fourth-grade classroom to teach financial literacy. What happened to me when I saw that banker in a classroom? It changed my life. Today, I am also an entrepreneur, and my organization Operation HOPE is a community banker of sorts. The seeds for both of those roles were planted in that classroom that day.

What happens when kids today see me as an entrepreneur talking to them about business? Aren't they going to want to model that too? What if they did model that—at scale?

I have told this story before, but for the newly introduced I offer the short version. It was around 1977. The federal government had recently passed the Community Reinvestment Act (CRA), which requires banks insured by the FDIC (Federal Deposit Insurance Corporation) to make efforts to invest, lend, and service underserved and low- to moderate-income communities like my own. The class was called Home Economics, and this banker was there to explain how life worked. He was Caucasian and was wearing a blue suit, a white shirt, and red tie. He was from Bank of America, the same bank where I opened my first bank account years later. (Know that these two things are connected in my story—in everyone's story, actually.)

For the first couple of financial literacy sessions, we didn't really know what to make of this banker, nor of the information he was sharing with us. I realized that the only other white people I knew in Compton were the principal of the school, my teacher, and a police officer in my community. The only white man I had ever seen in a suit was a police detective, and that suit was a cheap suit. But this banker's suit was obviously expensive. And he had a nice car in the parking lot.

I could not figure this guy out because the only "rich and successful" people I had met in my neighborhood were drug dealers and gang members. But this guy was calm, transparent, clean in dress and demeanor, and seemingly straight as an arrow. His money seemed legally earned.

During our third financial literacy session, I asked him an audacious question—although it seemed totally logical to me at the time. His answer changed my life.

"Sir, what do you do for a living, and how did you get rich, legally?"

You see, no one in my neighborhood wore suits. No one in my neighborhood was on a salary; they were all hourly workers. No one in my neighborhood had a business card. There were no tall, multi-floor office buildings other than the Compton courthouse. This man was like a Martian to me.

So I asked the question that was obvious to everyone who saw what I saw in our community. I was just the only one bold enough to open my mouth.

The banker responded, "Young man, I am a banker, and I finance entrepreneurs."

It was like a bolt of lightning hit me in the head out of the clear blue, and my life would never be the same. I said in response, "Well sir, I don't know what an entrepreneur is, but if it's legal and you're financing them, then I am going to be one."

I then went home and opened up the dictionary to the word "entrepreneur." It's a French word that loosely translates to "building something from nothing." That was what I wanted to be and it is who I am today.

Why do brilliant kids from the neighborhood end up becoming neighborhood drug dealers worth just $100 or $1,000 versus becoming the founders and CEOs of $1 billion global pharmaceutical companies? They have both the intelligence and the outsized entrepreneurial potential, so why the different choices? Easy: they are simply modeling what they see.

If the symbols of success you see in your neighborhood are rap stars, professional athletes, drug dealers, and gangsters, then why is anyone surprised that these are the people you grow up wanting to be? (And note there are only a few hundred wealth-building rap star slots to be had, and as for professional athletes, there are about 450 players in the NBA and 150 of those slots are filled with international players; in addition, most have an average playing time of only three to five years, and more than half of those that make it file for bankruptcy within five years of retirement.) But it's common sense, actually. We model what we see. The survivors in America, the groups that have been systematically left behind, need better role models.

After that life-changing conversation with the banker, I began to see my childhood community differently. I realized I had role models for wealth right in front of me. My father, who by then had owned a business for ten years. My mother, who had two side hustles and owned real estate. And now this banker, who showed me how to access large sums of capital on the same terms used by the most successful people in the country, most of whom happened to be white.

I saw the corner liquor store, Mac's Liquor Store, as a business, not just a place at which to buy stuff. And I saw the owner, Mr. Mac, as a black business owner, and thus another indirect role model. He was yet another amplification of what was possible for me.

Thanks to my parents pouring self-esteem into me, I also had the audacity and confidence to approach almost anyone with my opinions, thoughts, and dreams. And so I approached Mr. Mac.

I told him that from my "market knowledge" he was selling the wrong candy. He told me to go away, that he had a college degree and knew everything that he needed to know about running a business. I told him that I had cavities from eating candy, and that I knew everything that I needed to know about what kids actually ate—and thus, what sold (and what did not). He looked at me like I had three heads for daring, at age ten, to challenge his knowledge and wisdom. But he was also impressed, so he offered me a job manning the candy counter. I turned him down.

In this interaction Mr. Mac saw only my gift for talking, so he smartly wanted to sign me up to represent the candy sales counter in his liquor store. He told me it was the best job in his entire store. I respectfully turned him down, twice. I told him that I wanted to be his box boy, working in what they called the cold box, the back room behind the doors where the inventory was kept, including cold beer and drinks. I wanted to be the one moving the inventory. It was 45 degrees in that room. Mr. Mac had no idea why I would want to work there, earning minimum wage.

I wanted to do that job because my mind was focused on wealth-building, not check-cashing. I wasn't focused, then or now, on making money or getting paid, like almost everyone I grew up around was. I had my sights focused on a higher aspiration: ownership.

I learned early that you never wanted to be Blockbuster Video—at least, not by that name exactly. At one time, Blockbuster owned the market on dramatic consumer content entertainment. (Friday date-night at home meant getting to Blockbuster before everyone else!) But Blockbuster got over-confident and cocky. They had a chance to buy upstart Netflix for little to nothing, but turned it down. Today, Blockbuster is gone; Netflix owns the market on dramatic consumer content entertainment. I didn't have a name for it back then, but I knew I wanted to be the Netflix of my neighborhood. Let Mr. Mac be the Blockbuster.

I wanted that box boy job because it allowed me to see firsthand the candy Mr. Mac was ordering, what was moving, and what was not. And the reality confirmed what I already knew. He needed a software upgrade on his business, and he needed some competition. I offered the former and he rejected it, so I decided to become the latter. And so I quit and started my own candy business. The rest is history.

Anyone who hangs around me for any length of time

quickly comes to recognize how much I believe in the institution of mentoring and role-modeling. My mentors and role
models made me the man I am today.

Rev. Cecil "Chip" Murray was pastor of First AME Church
in South-Central Los Angeles, which had become the com-
mand center and the staging area for the black community's
response following the Rodney King riots of 1992. Rev. Murray told me many things, and this was the most important:
"John, it's not what people call you but what you answer to
that's important. And never, ever answer out of your name."
(You can learn much more about Rev. Murray in my book
Love Leadership: The New Way to Lead in a Fear-Based World.)

After graduating from the Rev. Murray school of integrity-
rich leadership, I decided to search out black men who happened to also be international role models. Unfortunately, I
could only find two examples at that time: music producer
Quincy Jones, and ambassador and civil rights icon Andrew
Young. I decided that I was going to become familiar with
both and that they would know me in return. The only problem was I didn't know either, and they couldn't care less
whether they knew me or not. And yet, I had decided that I
would change all of that, because I had decided early on that
I was worth it. You see, I believe in the James Brown version
of affirmative action: open the door, and I'll get it myself.

If people hear that they "ain't nothing," and that they're
"never going to be nothing," then they believe that, they live
that. But if I come along, and supposedly I "wasn't nothing,"
but I earn "something," even "a lot of something"—then
maybe people will begin to believe they can too. They can

be something and do something, something BIG, bold, and audacious. That's the power of role-modeling.

What do you think the winners are modeling for their next generation?

My wife Chaitra and I have the honor and pleasure of attending a couple of important meetings in different parts of the country each year. These meetings are typically made up of extremely wealthy and accomplished entrepreneurial builders, pioneering CEOs, and legacy wealth families.

But these gatherings are not business conferences or related to anything business—or related to anything in particular, really. There are no agendas, and no intentional business gets discussed. Actually, it's seen as rude to schedule a "business meeting" of sorts at these gatherings. But that doesn't mean that they aren't strategic.

Often these are multigenerational gatherings—so, not only are Mom and Dad getting to know the other X, Y, and Z individuals in their similar success lanes, but their children and grandchildren are also hanging out in their respective lanes. This is quality relationship-building and relationship-capital building like no other. And it is brilliant. Just like a contained university environment, at the same time each year, for a few days, these young people get to grow up together.

So here is my question. While these young people—the children of the accomplished builders—are there hanging out with each other, growing up with each other for a few days, twice a year; learning to trust and confide in each other; and then, ultimately, dreaming up stuff together—wouldn't you think it would be quite natural for these same young people when they become adults to want to invest in some ventures together? I certainly do.

Working with your wealth-building contacts is as natural for these young entrepreneurs as is walking with one foot placed in front of the other. And it comes about completely organically, which is why it works. And it is as old as the ages. This, ladies and gentlemen, is but one illustration of how the wealthy stay that way: with zero malice intent toward anyone else—and why the poor stay likewise.

Who you become depends on who you hang around.

Access for All

Education, the numbers of money, family structure, self-esteem and confidence, and role models: these are the factors that determine success or failure, on an individual level as well as within a neighborhood, a community, a town, a state, and a country. If any of us lacks more than three of those five factors, it's going to be really hard to climb that mountain called life's aspiration and emerge victorious on the other side. Not impossible. Just damn hard.

I want us all to win, and that means figuring out how each stakeholder in America can have access to these five pillars. They shouldn't have access just because they are lucky, like I was. They should have access as part of an established formula for winning.

CHAPTER 5

Capitalism for All

When my father was growing up, it mattered whether your neighborhood was primarily black or primarily white. Unfortunately, whether you grew up on the "wrong side of the tracks" or not was a huge determinant in your future success—or lack thereof.

Today, the details that matter for both someone's current life and their aspirations for the future has more to do with zip code than with race. In many ways your zip code helps to define your cultural code, your cultural DNA.

At Operation HOPE, working closely with analytics company FICO, we have collected data from two hundred metropolitan statistical areas (MSAs) and broken down the community characteristics tied to them. Here is the most startling commonality we found.

Almost all legitimate wealth—that didn't come from crime or war—originated from poor people. Even the "old money" originated from poor people; it's generational wealth built by immigrants who came here poor but whose children and their children's children were able to grow. I've previously mentioned Goldman Sachs; well, Marcus Goldman and Samuel Sachs started as two poor guys. Walmart began as a five-and-dime discount variety store started by a money-strapped Sam Walton.

But we seem to have forgotten this fact about America: that the way we have risen in the past, and that the only way we will rise in the future, is by supporting the next generation of entrepreneurship. It's time to reinvigorate the uniquely American entrepreneurial spirit, to double down on small business and restore this path to dignity. Everyone would have an entrepreneurial mindset if they believed they *could* succeed. Let's restore that belief.

When it comes to the poor coming up from nothing—the true promise of capitalism and of the American Dream—Atlanta is a model city, not just for the South, but for the entire nation. That's one of the major reasons why I live here and chose to found Operation HOPE here. Let me break down why.

Atlanta: A Model of American Capitalism

Atlanta, Georgia, is arguably the moral center of the United States of America. Atlanta was at the center of the American civil rights movement; it was the home base of some of the movement's pioneers: Rev. Ralph Abernathy, Rev. William Holmes Borders, Rev. Dr. Martin Luther King Jr., Coretta

Scott King, Congressman John Lewis, Rev. C. T. Vivian, Jean Childs Young, and Rev. Andrew Young, to name but a few.

Atlanta is the only city in the American South to host the Olympic Games. It is also home to the most black-owned businesses in the nation. It is one of the top ten fastest growing metropolitan statistical areas (MSAs) in the entire country; its airport is the busiest in the world.

The most effective integration of race, creed, class, and gender happens in Atlanta. The churches, colleges, government, and business community—all working together—created a true magic sauce. But the backstory of Atlanta is even more interesting than these impressive facts.

Atlanta walked through her deep, intense racial challenges to ignite her true renaissance, to turn her dream of shared economic progress into the reality of opportunity and prosperity for all.

Today Atlanta is the only international city in the South, but this outcome was far from promised or even dreamed of. Back in the 1950s, the city of Atlanta was dealing with the same small-minded "white versus everybody else" racial challenges that permeated the entire region. What made Atlanta different is how her people responded to this challenge, this distraction from her business plan.

Compared to other MSAs in the South, it's a big surprise that Atlanta came up as the region's sole international city and undisputed economic leader. Booming industrial revolution era economic powerhouses like Birmingham, Alabama, and Memphis, Tennessee, had more of a natural claim to this title. Both were geographically bigger with larger populations; their histories and storylines suggested they would rise ahead of Atlanta.

The vast majority of major and minor cities of the South were focused on—obsessed with, actually—the racial colors of black and white, and had taken very definitive and public stands around the issue. Mostly negative, low frequency, narrow stands. Let's say they had a surviving mentality. It was about putting up walls and barriers and separating. It was about controlling an old narrative and rejecting any future ones.

And then you had Atlanta. Ultimately, Atlanta decided to not argue about skin color or separating and barring; instead she focused her energy on how white and black folks alike could share the green.

Without question, there were and still are deep and troubling racial challenges in Atlanta. But Atlanta's city leaders did one majorly powerful and economically wise thing right: they decided that the real color worth debating about was not black or white, but green, as in US currency. It was the right fight.

Fighting the Right Fight

In the 1950s and 1960s, Atlanta leaned in on desegregation—late, but firm.

In the 1970s, Atlanta leaned in early on public transportation, which disproportionately serves low-income folks, setting a standard for the rest of the South.

In the 1970s and 1980s, Atlanta bet on Wall Street and won.

To back up a bit, in 1964, Atlanta native Dr. Martin Luther King Jr. won the Nobel Peace Prize for his nonviolent campaign against racism. Atlanta mayor Ivan Allen Jr. organized a celebratory dinner for Dr. King, but business leaders in Atlanta refused to honor the great civil rights leader. They had no interest in him whatsoever.

There was one leader, however, who thought differently. He saw himself and the company he ran as winners. He wasn't going to let racial divides mess with his business plan. That person was J. Paul Austin, then president of the Coca-Cola Company, which has headquarters in Atlanta.

Mayor Ivan Allen went to J. Paul Austin to explain that the business community was boycotting Dr. King's celebratory dinner and that anything less than a sold-out event would be an international embarrassment to the city. It did not take Mr. Austin long to move to action. Together, Mr. Austin and the mayor visited Robert W. Woodruff, former president of Coca-Cola and major philanthropist in the city, and together all three agreed that the event had to be a success. For the city to win, all her leaders needed to stand together in support of Dr. King.

J. Paul Austin pulled together a meeting of the city's business leaders and lay down what at that time must have been an unprecedented challenge to the city's leadership. His exact words: "Coca-Cola cannot stay in a city that's going to have this kind of reaction and not honor a Nobel Peace Prize winner."[1]

Now this would have been a serious power move for a business leader in 2020, but it was nothing short of extraordinary in the American South of 1964. And it worked.

Bolstered by Coca-Cola, the leadership emerging out of Atlanta's racist past decided that racism was not good for business. Atlanta always saw itself as a big league city. That also meant being a desegregated city without a lot of conflict. This remarkable example of how Atlanta's business leaders came together to focus not on the white or black but the green is part of what made the city the model for capitalism it is today.

Atlanta was the first city to do a mass transit referendum in the late sixties. It passed with the help of two largely minority-populated counties, Fulton and DeKalb, by just four hundred votes.

In order to win those counties, political leaders proposed a deal that introduced affirmative action to the South. They said that between 20 and 30 percent of all contracts for mass transit would go to minority drivers, managers, and businesses. The deal also lowered bus fare from 55 cents to 15 cents for ten years to appeal to the low-income populations in Fulton and DeKalb.

Atlanta also embraced the surge of blacks entering politics following Dr. King's assassination in 1968. There were not enough white people in the majority at that time to move the city in the right direction, so the progressive white leadership group became intentional, inviting successful black businessman Jesse Hill Jr. and others to integrate the chamber of commerce, the commerce club, and elsewhere of import in the city.

One of these political aspirants was the charismatic May-nard Jackson, who became the first-ever black vice mayor under Sam Massell, and then the first-ever black mayor in any major city in the South.

Wall Street was being integrated when Maynard Jackson took over in 1973, and he used his solid relationships to raise money for Atlanta so she wasn't dependent on only taxpayer funds. This strategy has paid enormous dividends, financing the airport and the new multibillion-dollar Centennial Yards project today.

Mayor Jackson also pioneered the responsible and legal use of public-purpose capitalism and merit-based opportunity sharing, effectively creating the black business wealth class in Atlanta during his two terms as mayor.

The wins just kept on coming to a progressive Atlanta. Entrepreneurial businessmen Arthur Blank and Bernie Marcus launched the Home Depot in 1980 as a start-up. Over the next twenty-five years, both became multi-billionaires. Both left Los Angeles for better opportunities in Atlanta, just like I would do years later myself. And while I may disagree with some of his politics, Bernie built one of the most meaningful companies in America today—up from nothing.

In 1972, pastor Andrew Young became the first black man since Reconstruction elected to the House of Representatives. After serving for two terms, in 1977 he was appointed United States Ambassador to the United Nations by President Jimmy Carter. Thereafter, his credentials and his relationship capital encompassed the world map. This clout served him well when, in 1982, he became mayor of Atlanta. Mayor Andrew Young reimagined the recession the nation was facing as an opportunity in disguise, and set out to bring in money from abroad. Lots of it. In the eight years he was mayor, Rev. Young brought in more than 1,100 companies and $70 billion of foreign direct investment. He created one million jobs for Atlanta.[2]

Mayor Andrew Young also helped get Georgia's Route 400 expressway approved, which is now the key artery between the wealthy Buckhead community and midtown Atlanta. He made this happen by holding over seventy community meetings in mostly white neighborhoods. He did this because he believed in himself, and he believed it was a winning proposition, and that belief bore out.

A decade later, Young brought the Olympics to Atlanta—and, with it, billions in revenue and untold prosperity. He had dreamed of going to the Olympics since he was four years old. Then, as an adult, he brought the Olympics to himself.

With no money to back up his dream, Young got Georgia Tech to draw up a vision for a proposed Olympic City. Young and his collaborators put it all in a book. Their vision was so compelling that everyone who reviewed the plan actually thought that everything in the book already existed. Then Young set out to sell the idea to the rest of the world. Calling on his many international connections, he wooed the votes of delegates from over one hundred countries. (More on the importance of relationship capital coming up next.) On September 19, 1990, in Tokyo, Japan, Young—and Atlanta—won the Olympic vote.

Now Young had six years to build their vision, but again no money with which to do so. So he approached then mayor of Los Angeles Tom Bradley, another of my early mentors, who encouraged Young to not use any public funds. Think about this. A public official, a mayor of a major city, encouraged another public servant and former mayor not to use public funds to put on the Olympic Games. Crazy, wasn't it? No, it was pure genius.

Mayor Bradley partnered with successful businessman Peter Ueberroth, also a friend and another early mentor for me; and Mayor Young partnered with successful businessman Billy Payne in Atlanta. Together, they raised $2.5 billion in private funds for the Atlanta Games.

Atlanta today thrives on its diversity. It sees diversity as a strength, both racially and economically. This is what you call a win-win plan. Today, Atlanta is as diverse as the United Nations itself.

Today, Georgia Tech graduates more black and Hispanic engineers than any educational institution in the world. Today, Georgia State University graduates more African Americans than any college or university in the world. More than one thousand black graduates enter the economy every year.

The HBCU (historically black colleges and universities) campuses of Spelman College, Clark Atlanta University, and Morehouse College share a rich 150-year heritage of a highly educated and ambitious black population working and growing up with the white population from the pre-existing privilege class. Almost every black scholar in American history has taught at one time or another in one of these three campuses. These HCBUs are the foundation of Atlanta's thought leadership.

For generations, black men and women in Atlanta have been fulfilling their dream of wanting to build great businesses, and of honoring their immense obligation and deep commitment to becoming civil leaders. It started with former slave and upscale barber Alonzo Herndon, who went on to create the largest black insurance company. His office, on Auburn Avenue and Peachtree Street, was where the black business community gathered back then. In 1906, Herndon was doing well enough that he personally financed the Niagara Movement, which in turn launched the vaulted NAACP in New York in 1909.

Atlanta expanded its vision beyond the state, beyond the South—even beyond the physical borders of the United States of America. Atlanta began to think as big as it was dreaming. Atlanta was the city that believed in itself, absent the arrogance and sense of entitlement that often comes with increased confidence.

Atlanta was blessed with many political leaders who were expert at articulating the business case for social change, including mayors Ivan Allen, Sam Massell, Maynard Jackson, and Andrew Young. Over the past seventy-plus years, Atlanta leaders decided they wanted Atlanta to be great. Not right, not superior, not anything else that would have detracted from their plans. They simply wanted to differentiate themselves from the rest of the (backward) South, and they succeeded.

All of these leaders were dreamers in disguise. You couldn't tell any of them what they could not do for the city. They all thought they were winners before they had won anything, before they had built anything, before they had become anything.

Though Atlanta believes in itself today, it was not always a winning city. Atlanta's leadership believed that it could be, and that made all the difference in the world. And now it stands as a shining example of what happens when we focus on the green and invest in our individual and collective uplift—and what happens when we invest in a capitalism for all.

Getting Staked (Relationship Capital for All)

Being smart, educated, and well put-together is not enough in 2020. Being "right" about something is not enough in 2020. Being deserving is no longer enough in 2020. Everyone feels like they are deserving today, whether that's true or not.

We have entered a world where everyone feels they have rights without assuming responsibilities for those rights. Those responsibilities start with self, then extend to loved ones and community. Social support is key. I believe that our US Congress should frame an incentives package for businesses and the wealthy that encourages them to commit to internship and apprenticeship programs at scale in exchange for generous tax write-offs. That's how we can stake the next generation and help them come up from nothing. When we exercise those responsibilities to better ourselves *and* our brothers and sisters, we become the reflection of this beautiful experiment that is America.

In the twentieth century, common people with uncommon determination and commitment advanced democracy and basic rights for all. This movement of civil rights leaders emerged in South Africa and featured Nelson Mandela and my friend Desmond Tutu, among others. Mahatma Gandhi fought for civil rights in India, as Michael Collins did in Ireland. In the southern states of America, the movement was led by Martin Luther King Jr., Andrew Young, Dorothy I. Height, John Lewis, and many others. These courageous efforts resulted in, among other things, the spread of real democracy in significant parts of the world and, ultimately, the right to vote for all. Because these civil rights leaders "staked" the unseen and the unheard, the lives of countless millions are better today. Empowered even. But that was the twentieth century; the twenty-first century is different.

In the twenty-first century, it's also important that you get staked. But today it's not only about the right to protest in the streets, it's also about the chance to do business in the suites.

Getting staked is an important part of this game called success. Getting staked is also what winners presume to be their birthright—not out of any sense of entitlement, as that would be obnoxious, but because they believe they are worthy of investment, belief, and backing by the best. Investments are what you make for the future, and someone staking you is one of the most powerful examples of investment.

Here's another success story out of Atlanta that illustrates my point. In 1970, Congressman Jim Howard of New Jersey was struggling for reelection. His district had been reapportioned such that he had new black constituents to appeal to. Two young black leaders, John Lewis and Andrew Young, stood up to campaign for him because they thought it was the right thing to do. They supported him because they liked his politics. And he won reelection—several terms over.

By the time Andrew Young became mayor, Congressman Howard had ascended to chairman of the transportation committee in the House. Though as representative of New Jersey he was more inclined to promote northeastern ventures, his relationship with and respect and appreciation for Andrew Young and John Lewis inspired him to authorize a major commitment of federal transportation money that triggered the development of I-75, I-85, I-20, and the start of the Perimeter in the city of Atlanta. (Interstate 285, which completely encircles the city of Atlanta is referred to as the Perimeter.)

As another example: telecommunication and entertainment entrepreneur Bob Johnson, who became the first African American to launch a $1 billion company in America, was staked at the onset of his business dream by telecommunications pioneering investor John C. Malone, who also was smart enough to turn a $120,000 equity investment into a nearly $700 million return on Johnson's BET network (BET being Black Entertainment Television). Now that's "doing well by doing good" on steroids!

Another stake story concerns my father-in-law, Dr. David Dalton, who established himself early on as a young builder of things. Dr. Dalton was originally staked by Alex Grass and Franklin Brown, who recruited and supported him as one of three executives that developed the original Rite Aid drugstore chain across America. Dr. Dalton rose to the number-three post of corporate vice president for the parent company, which he held from 1980 to 1989. Later, when Dr. Dalton decided to launch his own company, he was staked by a gentleman by the name of Mylan "Mike" Puskar, who was then CEO of Mylan Inc., a pharmaceuticals company. He invested the first $1 million into Dr. Dalton's ventures.

No one, nobody, rises to the top just on their own merit. I am honored to say that I have been staked by many amazing backers and endorsers over my time in business. That list includes Malibu restaurateur Harvey Baskin, Bishop Charles E. Blake, former Los Angeles mayor Tom Bradley, President George H. W. Bush, President George W. Bush, South African diplomat Sean Cleary, President Bill Clinton, civil rights icon Dr. Dorothy I. Height, entertainer Quincy Jones, First Horizon National CEO Bryan Jordan, Reverend Cecil "Chip" Murray, former SunTrust CEO Bill Rogers, Professor Klaus Schwab, Senator Diane E. Watson, civil rights icon Ambassador Andrew Young, and Ambassador Saburo Yuzawa of Japan. Most recently, I've been staked by Ares Management CEO Michael Arougheti and billionaire Tony Ressler. These names are part of the immense relationship capital that stood up and backed—and shouted the story of—one John Hope Bryant and Operation HOPE.

Before I close this chapter I'd like to share my memories of some of the first events and meetings I did with President Bill Clinton. When he focuses on you, it's as if you are the only person in the room. Prior to meeting President Clinton, I had built a personal relationship with one of his aides, Jena Roscoe, a brilliant mind and a caring heart who now works for me at Operation HOPE; and with the late Secretary of Commerce Ron Brown. Secretary Brown was special. At the time, he was arguably the highest-ranking African American in the US government, making him one of the most powerful individuals of African descent in the world. He could not have been a kinder person.

In order to keep up the momentum of our movement, I decided that I had to find a way to send a weekly update on our activities at HOPE. And so, either my chief of staff Rachael Doff or myself would stand at the fax machine from 7:00 to 9:00 PM, every Friday, feeding the machine with the seventy-odd letters, press releases, press clippings, or whatever else came in that week that bolstered our work. We sent our update to a targeted VIP list that always included Secretary Brown. Here's the real pain point: we had to manually punch in each and every fax number to each and every recipient each and every week. Talk about commitment. And talk about annoyance—on the receiving end.

Imagine walking into your office on Monday morning to find a pool of curled-up thermal paper (plain paper fax machines were not yet a thing) from John Hope Bryant all over your equipment room floor. Secretary Brown's staff pretty much hated me, as did the staff teams of pretty much every leader I dealt with back then, because all two-hundred-plus of them swept up my faxes every Monday.

But...all of this "annoyance" also meant that, whenever I

saw Secretary Brown, he was well informed about our latest work and activities, so I was top-of-mind whenever opportunities came across his desk that might apply to Operation HOPE. And that awareness led to some key introductions, endorsements, valuable relationship capital, and event grants for our work. Unfortunately, Secretary Brown's life was cut short in a tragic airplane crash in Croatia, Eastern Europe. Thirty-four lives were lost in that crash—and I lost a dear friend and mentor.

Later, Jena Roscoe explained to me that Secretary Brown had kept a detailed file on me, and Jena had been directed to maintain that file and keep in contact with me. In other words, I had gained entry to his club and, through him, access to President Clinton.

I don't know why President Clinton chose to stake me, but I am so very glad that he did. His engagement in my professional life, early on, advanced what I was trying to do. During his first weeks as a former president, he showed up in an Operation HOPE classroom in Harlem, New York, to teach financial literacy. He included me in his best-selling book on service and giving. Later on, he would help me solve a political challenge.

Everything is a club. Who in your club will stake you? Who will you stake? This is a key part of how we all come up. When we shift our mindset from individual to group success, we open up the relationship capital that allows us all to rise.

CHAPTER 6

Our Mental Upgrade as a Nation

I understood something important at an early age: if you are born black in America, then you are born on probation in America. In other words, this world is not going to cut you a break, and no one is going to give you the benefit of the doubt. You will have to step into your greatness—and remain there until your adversaries tire of trying to trip you up.

What I learned early on is that the best response to this injustice is not to get angry or to get even, but to decide that success is the best revenge. The world is the way it is until it isn't, and the way to change it is to win. That means you have to decide that you are going to win, no matter what obstacles and challenges you encounter.

That is the burden placed on the surviving class in America. It's not fair, but it is real. We can complain, we can focus on the negative—or we can do something about it. That's what I'm trying to do.

I'm trying to get the message across that it is in every American's interest that every American believes that they can win and that they have access to the tools for winning: the five pillars.

This is the mental upgrade we need, both individually and as a nation. This is the business plan for success for us all. We have to ignore the noise on all sides so we can focus on winning. We have to stake each other in order to fix the ladder, and we have to bet on us as a nation. This is how we all win.

Ignoring the Noise

During my entire life growing up and well into my thirties, and even my early forties, I was written off as an intellectual lightweight, as not a serious contender. I'm talking obvious eye-rolling by senior staff at the White House. I'm talking being referred to as nonsubstantive when within earshot, being waved away with a gesture that suggested I was not relevant to any important agenda.

These experiences developed into a life understanding for me. I decided it was more important to me to be respected than to be liked. I decided I would rather you respect me and learn to like me, than to like me but never respect me.

My mother taught me good manners, so I went out of my way to not be rude or disrespectful. But no matter how I behaved, clearly my actions promoting mainstream personal economic empowerment of the poor and the underserved were unnerving for many within the power dynamic. And so, I needed a different "response" to the challenge. Being a good person, or a competent person, was no longer enough. Moving from a surviving to a thriving mindset was no longer sufficient. I had to have a winner's mindset, and I had to wear it as if it were the daily armor of the Knights of the Round Table. I had to forget the noise so I could focus on winning.

In 1998, I was named the first-ever United Nations Conference on Trade and Development goodwill ambassador to the United States of America. A few years after, one senior staffer in the Clinton White House looked me straight in the eyes as he shook my hand and called me "Mr. Ham-bassador."

Obviously it hurt, because I remember the slight to this very day. But though it hurt my feelings, it had zero effect on my self-esteem, my self-confidence, my self-anything. In fact, I don't think I even responded to the gentleman. I simply heard what he said and filed it in my mental file cabinet. I already knew that my continued success was the best way to demonstrate the relevance of my message of empowerment. His unkind words were a distraction, and I wasn't about to be distracted from my business plan. All these years later, I'm still here and he is, well, literally gone off the scene. Nonrelevant.

It's important to note here that I'm not telling this story from a vicious or arrogant place. This isn't grandstanding. As a wise man once told me, "When you've got the power, you don't need to use it." I don't use my relevance for emotional gains. I don't get emotional because I learned that any decision I make emotionally is going to be a bad one. I ignored the White House staffer's noise so I could think and *respond* to the challenge, not react to it. I stepped over the mess he was trying to create for me, not in it. And that meant not being messy myself, because detractors love manipulating the mess in your life.

Playing at the levels that I was playing on—and at the levels I wanted to play on to achieve wins for the underserved—meant that I needed to steel myself to criticism. I developed a mindset, a mental toughness, an emotional maturity, and an internal resiliency that would allow me to simply wave away even the most stinging personal rebuke. As long as any comment wasn't true in my soul, it didn't much matter what anyone else had to say. Those who win do so because they stay in the game and never give up. Fear and failure are lazy bastards who don't like to do the real work of life.

I learned from one of my mentors, Rev. Cecil "Chip" Murray, that it's not what people call you, it's what you answer to that's important. So I never, ever answer to anything but my name. In addition, I learned that to argue with a fool only proves that there are two—and that's why I ignore the noise.

And that's what we all need to do, individually and as a nation. We need to ignore the noise of division and name-calling and finger-pointing and shaming, because none of it matters. What matters is that we know who we are: America, the land of freedom and opportunity for all; and we have a plan for what we want to accomplish in this world. Let's plan to win.

Our Plan for Winning: No "Buts"

The plan for winning is simple. For the first twenty-five years of Operation HOPE, I told my team to never do anything that they didn't want to see on the front page of the *New York Times* in five years.

I told them:

Don't buy me a first-class plane ticket. I'll upgrade from coach with either earned points or my own wallet.

Don't put me in a limousine, even if it's the only vehicle available at two in the morning. I'll take a cab.

Don't book me into a five-star über-luxury hotel unless someone else is paying for it and there's a real reason to do so.

These rules worked for me for the first twenty-five years because during that time I was aiming for survival. I wanted to move from surviving to thriving, and now that box is checked.

Once I'd moved the goal post, the mentality had to be one of winning. From that day forward, I went by a different rule: that my name or my work would never be followed by a "but…" When I leave a meeting, I want the person I was meeting with to not say, on substance or merit:

"You know, I would love to work with John, but…"

"I'd be happy to support and partner with Operation HOPE, but…"

"I really admire what John Hope Bryant is doing, but…"

Now, if the "but" was personal, meaning they just didn't

like the way I looked, walked, talked, or whatever, that wouldn't bother me at all. It's everyone's God-given right to like or not like whomever they want. But what I could not and would not tolerate was to be denied on *merit*.

And so, my new objective with respect to how I run my world, including my organization's financials, is this: be as clean as the pope's robe. If that's covered, then I can say what I like and do what I want. That's called freedom. And so, that's precisely what I did.

Recently, we discovered that an auditor had done less-than-perfect work for us. It wasn't malicious or even incompetent, but it left me open to critics and criticisms. And yet, we spent zero time arguing about the misfortune of the whole thing, or how we didn't deserve what was being served up as the product of our own doing. We ignored all that noise. We simply moved on to a new audit firm, who simply redid two years of audits.

The result: the new audits showed the organization was in better shape than the original audits had. Among other findings, rather than 82 cents of every incoming dollar going directly into programs, we saw that figure move to 87 cents. We picked up a few million dollars in registered unrestricted income, and retained our standing as a four-star Charity Navigator–rated organization in the top quartile of all nonprofit organizations in the nation.

No "buts."

This is a really important point to appreciate for leaders-in-the-making, especially those who come from historically disadvantaged groups. It's about not giving "them"—those with the power to lift you up or break you down—any reason to do the latter. It's about playing their game, and playing it well, so that you earn their respect—not necessarily their love or even their like, but definitely their respect.

Here's another example. Everyone's hero, Dr. Martin Luther King Jr., had an incredible sense of humor and he was incredibly cool around his closest friends, but he also knew that no one was going to give him the benefit of the doubt. He knew that he would be under a microscope with every move that he made. As a result, Dr. King would not wear sunglasses, he would not smoke cigarettes in public (there is only one photo recorded with him ever doing either), nor would he joke around in public. He didn't want anyone writing him off as a leadership lightweight. He didn't want to give anyone the ammunition to discount him. He wanted "no buts" in his life, and that included cigarette butts.

My father-in-law, Dr. Dalton, operates the same exact way. He knows that not managing the details tightly is how professionals in the health care space get walked off the field, so to speak. So Dr. Dalton makes sure that he has all the credentials, approvals, renewals, licenses, permits, and even patents needed for him to sit at the big table of aspirational achievement in his field. There can be no "buts" about his or his company's competency. If you don't like him, that's okay, but you absolutely cannot say he doesn't run a top-notch office. You can't say he's not in compliance. His immaculate reputation and operations are also a source of self-esteem and self-confidence. When he leaves a meeting—contract or no contract, opportunity or no opportunity—he remains Dr. David Dalton, a winner.

We May Be Down, but We're Never Out

After I closed my candy store, my next series of businesses as a young entrepreneur were a collection of consulting hustles, marketing plays, and product-placed businesses—and the one thing consistent among them all was failure. Most of my next ventures simply didn't work. But that was okay, because I had become hooked on the aspirational currency of my own dreams, my passion for building something. From Stacy Adams shoes, to Omni Jewelry, to whatever happened to catch my imagination during that sales period, I was representing and showing up. My father-in-law always reminds me that half of success is showing up, and he is right. I knew the *what* was entrepreneurship for me; now I just needed to learn the *how*. The real success at this stage of my business career and life was my resiliency. I simply never gave up, gave in, or allowed anyone—and I mean *anyone*—to define me. As I like to say, I took all those "no's" as my vitamins.

I went on to attend Whaley Middle School in Compton, California. By this time, my mother knew I wanted to be a businessman, and she wanted me to dress the part so I could see myself in that image. But she could not afford to buy me a business wardrobe on her hourly salary as a fabricator at an aircraft production company. She was a single mother by then. So Mom went to Plan B: she decided to make the suits she thought I needed herself. The only one of these suits I actually remember was a purple, crushed-velvet-and-suede, three-piece suit with a ruffled shirt, and a big, big, big bow tie. I wore that suit and, with my briefcase filled only with my wishes, hopes, and dreams, trundled off to Whaley. In Compton.

I got my rear end wiped every single day at that school.

The tough guys at school assumed that, if I was bold enough to wear clothes like that to this school, I must have some money. They were going to take that money they thought I had or break my independent spirit trying. (Their other desire was to have me and every other kid in my neighborhood join their gang and I simply would not. I wasn't hating on what they were doing. It just was not for me, that's all.) But like iron toughening iron, the more they beat me up, the tougher and more resilient my inner spirit and inner fortitude became.

And so, there I was. Hustling every day to make a way out of no way. I even tried my hand at the acting trade for a period, and this no doubt is where I learned how to communicate. It may also be where I honed my marketing skills. I had no trust fund. I had no backup plan. I didn't want to work for anyone else but me. I had an outsized view of my own God-given potential. And, later on, I would come to believe that I also had a public calling in my life—not political office, but the empowerment of the people at scale. To get there, I had to get through this period. My strong-as-steel winning mentality was forged entirely by adversity.

As I said in my book *Love Leadership,* "Success is all about successfully managing pain: the pain we create for ourselves, and the pain visited upon us by others." Success in life is not about what happens to you; it's about how you choose to respond.

It's hard for someone else to call me a jerk when I acknowledge that I am probably one unconsciously and unintentionally, every Tuesday for two hours. I fully acknowledge that every day, or certainly every week, I am part eagle, buzzard, and unfortunately, turkey (profiling a bit still) too. We are works of art, always in progress. But the goal is not perfection, but rather progression.

I had a mobile car-detailing business. It ultimately failed.

I ran a concert promotions company. It ultimately failed.

I started a Fila-Ellesse marketing business. It ultimately failed. This one deserves a little background.

Growing up, everyone in my neighborhood wanted to wear Fila and Ellesse sportswear, but most could not afford those brands. As we all know, challenges create opportunity, and the opportunity for most urban entrepreneurs was a little merchandising "misrepresentation." Said bluntly, they made and sold fraudulent Fila and Ellesse goods in the hood.

Since the raids on these sweatshop operators and sellers was constant and predictable, I thought their business plan was, well, simplistic. So I decided to look around a bit—in legal books! And what I found, by looking in places that others were not looking, was that both brands held franchise licenses in Brazil, Italy, USA, and Mexico. *Mexico,* I thought, *well that's less than two hundred miles from here . . .* So I jumped in my car and drove to Mexico. (By this time I was in my late teens, and I did have a car, but there was no way I could afford to fly.)

What I found in Mexico blew my mind. Less than 250 miles from North America, the same products were selling for a fraction of the retail price. And these products were legit! I quickly discovered a loophole in the global licensing rules, and began marketing and selling legal Fila and Ellesse goods to anyone who would purchase them—anybody. My next not-so-smart move was walking into a couple Fila and Ellesse stores in Beverly Hills and Palm Springs, California, offering to sell them the same goods they were buying from whomever at a fraction of the US wholesale price.

The response to my bold offer was utter shock; they were stunned at my bravado, I guess. Soon, representatives from the two companies showed up at my "showroom" and purchased a couple of my tracksuits. But after that, I received a letter from what was then one of the largest law firms in America threatening to sue me for "unfair compensation." When I asked my newly retained lawyer what that meant, the response was a wry smile. Basically, it was explained to me, I beat the companies and the lawyers at their own game. I had exploited them with a gap I'd found in their overlapping licensing rules, and now they were shutting me down. If I didn't agree to go away, they would assign a battery of high-priced and high-powered lawyers to pursue me, draining me of every dollar I had and then some.

My lawyer advised me to take this as a win, sign the document, and move on before I really got hurt. So, even though

I failed, I won, so to speak, and would live to fight another (business opportunity) day.

Here's another interesting dimension to this story: to grow this little venture I had borrowed some funny money from a bad guy, a local gangster whose loan terms suggested that one would never repay him. (Meaning, I would be doing business with him for life.) But he was so impressed by what I had pulled off that he released me from this agreement-in-bondage. I guess he thought I had real potential, potential that even he wanted to see mined. I said thank you and kept it moving. This experience also taught me a valuable lesson about my "sources of funds" for the future. I became obsessed with becoming a "bank-qualified" borrower. I wanted to qualify for the best of the best, with the best of terms to match—and one day I would.

I must have tried one hundred different business concepts between age ten and age nineteen. I even ended up homeless for six months when I was eighteen. With my ever-changing array of new business ideas, I experienced time and time again what anyone else would call crushing failures, but to me they were all warm-up acts. They were just launching pads for my passion, energy, and ideas. They were opportunities—just not the right ones for me. And the one thing I never questioned in the midst of all of this was me.

I could not be prouder of my so-called defeats during that period of my life. I went down a lot, but I was never out. I lost many battles, but I won the war. The war of my own self-belief. The victory over my own self-doubt. It was the beginning of my resiliency-building story.

As someone pursuing a dream, you learn to take "no" for vitamins. That has been my story and that has been America's story since her birth as a nation. It's a story she needs all of us to continue. And the first step is never giving up on her dream.

Do Your Part to Fix the Ladder

When I was a young man coming up in business, I had the pleasure of being introduced to Los Angeles mayor Tom Bradley. Though he is a real giant in the Southern California political establishment, unfortunately his leadership era preceded the internet, so many in younger generations have never heard of the first black man elected to lead a major city, and who led it for twenty years.

Tom Bradley saw something in me and took me under his wing, allowing me relatively free rein of his City Hall complex. And while his support of me genuinely irked his closest aides, like Bill Elkins ("what the hell is that kid John Bryant doing around here again?"), others, such as Will Marshall and Bill Raphael, made sure that I was visited by, exposed to, and constantly engaging with the mayor. On one occasion, they even made sure I had a seat on a delegation with the mayor of South Korea.

To be clear, I had no ties with South Korea, but Will and Bill knew that smart, young African American men and women coming up had to be exposed to the international arena. So I went to South Korea. I gladly paid the costs associated with participating with the mayoral delegation, because what I was receiving in return was priceless: access to some of the top leaders from Los Angeles and from South Korea. Today I really feel for the LA leaders on that trip, because at the time I was relentless with my constant barrage of enthusiastic questions and proposals for working together.

Within a short time, I found myself volunteering on a number of key committees, boards, and task forces tied to the mayor and the city. I considered these roles my duty as a citizen and my service to Los Angeles—with the added bonus of finding myself, more often than I can remember, sitting next to CEOs and other influential business people. This was access and context that I could not pay for.

If I had previously tried to call any of those CEOs out of the blue, I never would have made it past the receptionist. But because I volunteered my time and agreed to lend my thought leadership to the same problems they were trying to solve for the city, I found myself in a working relationship with a number of high-level business leaders, right there next to me in those nonprofit and public service committee meetings! And they wanted to do good too!

Later on, my volunteerism morphed into genuine advising and counsel for the mayor and his administration. This led to my dreaming up a new small business and commercial lending agency, one that still exists to this day within Los Angeles. I dreamed it up, and the city officials loved the idea, but—as would prove the case time and again for many more years of my life, they thought I was too young to handle the reins. They simply took the idea I drafted, gave the credit to someone else, and let them run with it. And that was totally fine with me. I learned long ago from my best friend and advisor Rod McGrew that "fair exchange is no robbery." I benefited more than enough from my association with the Bradley administration. Plus, I was tickled pink that something out of my young mind had become an official city lending agency! In many ways, this first vision for Los Angeles was the precursor to what would later become Operation HOPE.

Today, I have 100,000 quality relationships spanning the globe, people who happily take my calls, be they in community rooms, school rooms, or corporate board rooms; corridors of city, state, or federal political power; or heads of state and royalty, the world over. And it all started with my volunteering my time in a couple dingy, rarely used conference rooms stuck up near the attic in Mayor Tom Bradley's City Hall.

Many of my first business relationships, the first investors in my dream, came from these experiences of volunteering to make my birth city of Los Angeles better. This was the beginning of building my relationship capital.

It started with my focusing on what I had to give in a world filled with people seemingly obsessed only with what they can get. And as my story shows, there is a moral responsibility to give but there is also the business case.

If the moral argument doesn't work for you, you still can't deny the business benefits. The business world is made up of people—how are you going to get them to remember who you are? What are you doing to get staked?

And at the country-wide level, what happens when you

help the people above and below you grow a bigger pie? How big would that pie be if every person in America had access to the same ladder, so they could come up from nothing?

Betting on US

I was once a member of a prominent national small business group out of Washington, DC, and I was one of very few blacks ever present at any of their meetings. While many of my friends would have found that to be a problem, I found it to be just fine. It would now be even easier for someone to remember me! Well, that worked out better than I imagined.

One day I was approached by an executive at one of the meetings. He had invited me to sit in the front row, I am convinced now, only because I was the only brother in the room. He had a problem he needed to solve and needed my help! The group was being recognized by then president George H. W. Bush, and they needed someone from the group for the president to highlight in his upcoming speech on the south lawn of the White House.

"Didn't you do a lot of volunteering in Los Angeles to help the less fortunate?" he asked me nervously. I confirmed that I did, and before I knew it I was recruited.

It turned out that the group needed an inspiring story of a business person who was giving back to society and community, whereas apparently the majority of their prominent members were solely focused on the art of making money for themselves. The group had found themselves in a pickle, and I was able to get them out of it.

Before I knew it, I was sitting in the front row of a presidential ceremony at the White House. I heard my name mentioned by a US president, and I will never forget that moment for the rest of my life. Here was the leader of the free world recognizing me for doing well while also doing good—indeed, recognizing me for the value of my life's work. What a long road from Compton and South-Central Los Angeles! Just as I found myself mentally rambling down memory lane, I snapped out of my reverie. President George H. W. Bush was walking past me. I got to shake his hand.

I didn't really know what to say, and then thought maybe saying something stupid actually wasn't so bad. I asked the man for his business card. The president of the United States of America. He looked at me, lovingly, like I had three heads, and then pointed upward, very nicely. "I live up there in the White House," he told me. "I'm easy to find."

Well, it might have been stupid, but it was memorable. I was hoping he'd never forget me and he did not. More importantly, others in the president's cabinet saw me in conversation with the president and presumed that I must be someone important. That, and the fact that he had just mentioned my name in his speech, made me golden—at least for twenty-four hours!

Twenty-four hours later I was back in my offices in Los Angeles, on the phone with Jack Kemp, the Secretary of the Department of Housing and Urban Development. Kemp was an incredibly charismatic and kind man. I asked for a fifteen-minute meeting and reminded his secretary that I was the young man that the president had just saluted in the speech at the White House. Being a prominent cabinet member, Secretary Kemp had been there. He'd know what I was talking about. I got my meeting.

Two or three days later, I was on a plane heading back to Washington, DC, an almost 6,000-mile round trip that would cost me several thousand dollars that I really didn't have. (I was already behind on the rent for my office suite in ritzy West Los Angeles.) Why DC again? For my scheduled fifteen-minute meeting with Jack Kemp—except he had no clue that I was coming.

Complicating matters further, I also had no clue what I wanted from him! All I knew was that God made me a winner, this was a once-in-a-lifetime opportunity, and I was going to roll the dice! I was going to bet on me, and on my ability to turn nothing into something. Once again. And the bet worked.

When I showed up in HUD Secretary Jack Kemp's office, he asked why I was back in town so soon. I told him I was only there to meet with him. I had flown 3,000 miles simply for a fifteen-minute meeting. That stopped Kemp and his chief of staff in their tracks—and that was my plan. Based on my research, I knew that Kemp was a decent man with a soft spot for those left behind, and I'd made a bet to myself that he could not knowingly allow me to come all that way without attempting to add a little protein to my diet dinner plate, so to speak. Soon I found myself being led throughout the entire HUD building, from one meeting to the next, shadowing the secretary.

The biggest part of that day's schedule was the swearing

in of Raoul Carroll, the first African American president of the Government National Mortgage Association (known as Ginnie Mae). Unfortunately for Mr. Carroll, I was there too. I say "unfortunately" because at the very moment he was about to be sworn in, Secretary Kemp inserted his own remarks, announcing that "his friend John Bryant was visiting from Los Angeles." (Everyone present that day believed that I was a friend of the Secretary!)

The next week I made a third trip from Los Angeles to DC, this time to meet with the newly minted Ginnie Mae president. Mr. Carroll didn't know what we were meeting about, but, like Secretary Kemp, he felt that he *should* meet with me. And so we met and, as luck would have it, an opportunity emerged for me to enter into a multimillion-dollar loan-servicing contract with Ginnie Mae—and GE Capital even agreed to finance the entire deal! All of this came together just weeks from that first meeting. As it happens, it also fell apart not long afterward, but that was actually a good thing too. All this happened in the summer of 1991. Soon after, it was obvious that President Bush would not be reelected, at which point GE Capital pulled out faster than you could ask "why?" I decided then and there that I was through with politically motivated deals—which is why it was ultimately a good thing. But that's not the point of my story.

Here is my magic sauce: I am super resilient. The response to the pain, the pounding, and the problems of life, is *the thing*. But I didn't start out this way. I used to be very, very delicate. I am a very sensitive individual. Super sensitive, actually, but I cover it well—because I was convinced early on that, if others knew, they would have played it and tried to use it against me. So I decided to "fake it until I made it."

As a young man coming up I had acquired high confidence from the high competence I demonstrated, starting with my Neighborhood Candy House business at ten years old. But for the two decades following that, I struggled with my self-esteem. What kept me going during those developing years was my mother's love. My mother told me that she loved me every day of my life, and this was my real inner wealth until I secured some of my own.

I was socially awkward in my early years, and so I turned inward for companionship, self-understanding, and self-belief. I remember being eight years old and walking through my neighborhood in Compton, California, twirling a pencil through my fingers, completely enthralled in the superhero drama series I was creating in my head. I was in my own world. I am sure that others in the neighborhood called my mother and sister to report me walking endlessly through the neighborhood, talking to myself, and wondering if I was okay, probably thinking I had a mental condition or something.

I was always an oddball, and early on I got used to being called out. But I had my mother's affirmation of love pouring into me daily—plus my sister Mara Lamont "Montie" Hoskin, who would beat up anyone who messed with her baby brother. I was covered, front, back, and center. I was safe to become myself—totally, fully, and completely.

From this and other outlier experiences coming up, including walking to school in three-piece suits and carrying a briefcase in inner-city Compton, I discovered that I was enough, all by myself.

First they ignore you. Then they criticize you. Then, when you begin to win, they start to copy you. And then—in time—you win.

Right now, we're the ones criticizing ourselves in America, and they're the ones benefiting—and yet, at the same time they're also trying to copy us. We are not betting on ourselves. But if we're not betting on ourselves, who are we going to get to bet on us?

I have a message to give you: RELENTLESS BELIEF. In yourself, in each other, and in US, the US of A.

Green Is How We All Win

If you want to see American aspiration at work, just follow the money. If you want to understand who wins and why, just follow the people with embedded confidence, self-esteem, and poured-in love. Optimism, hope, resiliency, authenticity of purpose and mission, and relentless hard work succeeded for me, even when most everyone around me hoped that it and I would fail.

Since the Rodney King riots of 1992, Operation HOPE, with now more than five thousand partners, has directed more than $3.5 billion in private capital into underserved neighborhoods and communities, supporting and assisting more than four million clients to date. The foundation has grown 553 percent over the past five years alone. It is the largest national for-purpose, nonprofit financial inclusion organization in America, with 150-plus HOPE Inside locations operating in twenty-two states, serving clients in forty states, and raising credit scores 54 points over six months, and 120 points over twenty-four-months' time.

My secret formula for success, and ultimately for winning at life, is that I am fed by the process, not the outcome. Not the goal line, because there is no goal line. Once a type-A-achiever personality gets to the so-called goal line, we're already focused on what's next. As it's often said, "the road to success is constantly under construction." It's about the process.

My next goal was to prove that we could achieve and accomplish in the private sector what we had done in non-profit space. I wanted to prove that doing good is good business. In 2017, I stepped back into my entrepreneurial shoes and founded a real estate company focused on single-family residential real estate. This company would combine the ownership of a portfolio of workforce housing—single-family residential homes in middle-class and working-class neighborhoods—with free financial literacy coaching and counseling through a paid contract from my new company to a nonprofit counseling organization. Residents who stayed with me for five years and paid on time would then enter a program designed to step them into responsible home ownership on their own terms. The new company was the Promise Homes Company.

Though the new company launched in June 2017, the backdrop of this exciting new business began almost a decade prior. Somewhere around 2008, I met Mr. Michael Arougheti, the brilliant young and respected CEO of $150-billion-asset Ares Management. I met him through what was then called the Financial Services Roundtable (FSR) organization, now the Bank Policy Institute (BPI). FSR was the collection of the largest one hundred bank and financial companies in the country, and the CEOs of these companies gathered once a year for their annual meeting. My life was changed when Don McGrath, then CEO of Bank of the West, suggested that I pay attention to this group of banking leaders. I did.

Don introduced me to the CEO of FSR, Steve Bartlett, and I made sure I said everything I needed Steve to hear in the short, eight-minute conversation we had. I figured, after eight minutes, if I had not connected with both sides of his brain—the right (aspirational and creative) and left (intellectual and factual)—then I would not connect at all. Luckily, I did connect with Steve, and as a result he let me into the FSR family, and all the doors for my future success flew wide open soon thereafter.

After Steve Bartlett, the next CEO of FSR was former Minnesota governor Tim Pawlenty. Side note: Governor Pawlenty was not one for blowhards—folks who are "all hat, no head." My sales skills would not help me with him. At the C-suite level, being a great salesman or marketer is not necessarily complimentary, so I had to learn the art of communicating crisp substance.

What followed for my nonprofit organization were powerful and, in many cases, first-ever partnerships that have stood the test of time. We have built signature partnerships with the likes of Bank of America, First Horizon Bank, JPMorgan

Chase, PNC Financial Services, Regions Bank, SunTrust Banks (now Trust Bank), Synovus, US Bank, Wells Fargo, and so many others. Genuine new friendships with CEOs like Jamie Dimon, Bill Rogers, and Bryan Jordan, among many others. And all of this came from a simple recommendation, a simple introduction, and my belief in myself as a winner well before I actually won anything.

From there I asked my now friend Michael Arougheti to join my board at Operation HOPE. We just clicked. Later on, Michael asked if I would consider joining the board of a newly launched, publicly traded commercial real estate investment trust (REIT) to be called Ares Commercial Real Estate. Michael and my now friend and business partner Tony Ressler were cofounders of the entire Ares world.

I had served on several corporate boards before, but somehow this one seemed different. Special. A potential gateway opportunity, perhaps, but I didn't know to what—or why I even felt that way. I let myself be led by faith. I showed up to every meeting as if only the best version of my brain was acceptable. I didn't want to be the token black director in the room; I wanted to be respected as one of the sharpest and most contributing directors in the room.

It was not always easy. I was new to the sector, the company, and the new space of public companies, and sometimes I made mistakes. Occasionally I showed up not as prepared as I would have liked—the pressures on me at Operation HOPE during that period were unrelenting—and my critics made sure to point that out. I just made sure to never get emotional, to never get angry, to always keep my cool. I walked right through whatever challenge or problem I found in front of me. Never giving up is one of my lifetime best qualities.

And there were directors who, let's just say, were not exactly my biggest fans either. I am a disruptor—albeit a positive one—and I perhaps drove traditionalists a little crazy. My response to all of that noise was simply to double down on me. I got better. I practiced choosing a positive response to negativity. Looking back, I think that Michael and Tony were paying attention. Maybe, possibly, they were watching how I responded to what was placed in front of me, checking out what I was really made of.

After working with Michael and his team there for a couple of years, he and I began talking about a possible opportunity in the single-family residential home rental sector. For the first couple of years that we batted around the idea, Michael was not all that interested. Michael is a genius for the numbers, and he thought the sector had too many unanswered questions to scale it into a business. That was his opinion until his opinion changed—and it takes a *lot* to change Michael's view on something. After a number of failed discussions, Michael and I finally agreed on what began as a fairly modest investment (modest for Michael, but fairly major for me).

A few weeks later I went to visit with Tony Ressler in Los Angeles, prepared to ask him (okay, beg him) for a $50,000 contribution to Operation HOPE. Tony said, "Okay, I am glad to help with a contribution, but what else do you have?" Translation: Charity is fine, but what business do you have to talk about? Do the business, and you'll have as much money as you like to give to the charity of your choice. Tony's was a lesson I would never forget.

I told Tony about the little business deal that Michael and I had dreamed up. It took him about three minutes of calculus in his mind to come to the same conclusion as Michael had: this could make a lot of sense. Tony wanted to be a partner too. I had learned early on: never say no to an honest billionaire.

Not so long after, on a conference call about this then-modest investment, Tony said, "Why do X, when you can do X times ten?" Now, if Michael is the numbers genius, Tony is the genius for building scale—and I mean *very* big scale. Within two years, we had scaled this dream. The help and unconditional support of Michael and Tony grew the Promise Homes Company from zero to $100 million in assets. That's 303 percent growth over that period. Today, we are negotiating a merger to scale up again, moving the company to the next level.

Now these two highly successful genius businessmen—successful as in they have built and managed more than $150 billion of business assets, real estate ventures, and responsible finance companies—never asked me for a PowerPoint presentation. They didn't ask me for a one-hundred-page business plan. They asked me fundamental questions about the business, and came to believe the sector was sound and presented opportunity. Most of all they trusted me. They wired money—lots of it—on faith and belief in me. And they liked me. (No one does business at this level unless they like and respect you.) They wanted me to win. But first, they had to believe that *I* believed I was a winner.

Someone once told me, "You don't buy companies or an asset list of desk and chairs and inventories; you buy management teams." Or, as my friend Herb Allen III of investment bank Allen & Company once told me, "We bet on the jockeys, not the horses in a race."

It's about the talent and the business plan.

In America, we have the talent. This country, built on the backs of up-from-nothing go-getters, has everything it takes to win. We just need to believe we can win. And we need a better business plan.

Conclusion

"**S**uccess has a thousand mothers, and failure is a bastard child," the old saying goes. Today when I travel back to Los Angeles, I receive nothing but kudos from friends and former foes who respect what we built and the contributions we made. And while I appreciate each and every person who shares their comments, I decided long ago that none of it would matter. I am just a man trying the best I can to become the best I can be. That will have to be enough. And it is enough for me. Through the founding struggles of Operation HOPE, I had been awarded the crowning achievement that important people the world over often never achieve: I had become reasonably comfortable in my own skin.

I realized much later in life that there had been a bonus for me in my experience with the white banker at nine years old. You see, before this experience, the only interactions I'd witnessed between white people and my black and brown friends in the neighborhood were negative. It was always some white police officer throwing a young black man against a car talking *at* him, seldom if ever *to* him. It was demeaning and dedignifying, and it set my black friends against police presence in my neighborhood. But my experience was different.

The principal of my elementary school was white, and she took a special interest in my success. (Thank you, Colin P. Kelly Elementary School, previously El Segundo Elementary.)

One of my best teachers was white, and she always bought whatever I was selling from my briefcase of mail-order-product hope. You see, back then I didn't have enough capital to even buy product samples, so I could only carry around mail-order catalogues, and had to "make the sale" through force of personality, stick-to-it-iveness, follow-up, and persistence.

The two managers at the local Thrifty Drug store in Compton, who caught me at age eight trying to steal crayons and took me upstairs to scare me straight—they were white too. They told me that if I ever tried that again, they would be watching for me on their cameras and they would send me to *prison*. They then explained, lovingly but firmly, how terrible and dehumanizing the prison experience would be for me. After my black face flushed white with fear, and my eyes grew as large as turnips, they opened the door to their upstairs office, and ever so gently allowed me to walk out. Free. I vowed to never, ever, steal anything ever again, and I never did. I vowed I would work for whatever I wanted, and I still do. And I thank both of these nameless, faceless heroes in my life.

And then there was that banker who showed up in my classroom when I was nine. He didn't seem to really want be there, and we didn't particularly want him there. But the federal Community Reinvestment Act made it so that his employer demanded he visit us. As a result, he realized these young black boys and girls were more like his own white, privileged, suburban kids than he'd thought. And we realized that he wasn't such a bad dude. Actually, he was a great guy, and my only regret is that I never got his business card. Because his taking just a little more time with me than was required changed my life, forever.

These positive experiences—with people, male and female, from another race, place, and socio-economic background— ensured that I was never intimidated by white folks, nor angry at them, nor uncomfortable around them. In fact, I was thereafter convinced that I deserved to sit right next to them in that corporate suite of my future.

From these experiences I learned that, whether you are an entrepreneur, an hourly worker, a doctor, artist, historian, or a PhD, the same reality holds true: we live in a free enterprise democracy. The color is green. It always has been. That's the business plan.

Andrew Ross Sorkin is a columnist for the *New York Times* and coanchor of Squawk Box, CNBC's morning business news show. At the *Times* he also founded the daily financial report DealBook. He has known me for a long time since his wife, Pilar Queen, is my book agent. For whatever reason Andrew took an interest in me and took a chance on me. Squawk Box had never had an African American regular anything on the show, and so he brought me on as a guest host not one time, not two times, not three, but more than twenty times.

The bet Andrew made is similar to the one that Tony Ressler and Michael Arougheti made on me: do good but also do well. In staking me, Tony and Michael said, *Look, we want you to make a lot of money, and maybe help to fund your mission with it, and we don't want to lose any money. The two have to go together.* And I have actually helped them to make some money while doing some good.

Similarly, Andrew told me I have to talk to those CEOs who watch Squawk Box in words they understand. My message of doing good for the underserved will fall on deaf ears if it doesn't also help their businesses do well.

Paraphrasing, this is what Andrew was trying to communicate to me: Talk to the audience so that it resonates. Meet them where they are so that they take your message without becoming defensive. Affirmative action and reparations may scare them; talking positively about your own view of capitalism will surprise them. Don't ramble on without being relevant, and don't embarrass yourself or me. But come and talk for three minutes and leave a powerful impression that will maybe expand their idea of capitalism to include giving a hand up to those on the bottom without their knowing that you're giving them an upgrade on their way of thinking.

And that's what I did. And now I have a regular guest-cohost gig on Squawk Box that is giving my mission and work added visibility and reach.

Andrew staked me and he didn't have to. So did Tony and

Michael. That is what each person in America needs to do if we actually want the freedom of opportunity for all. Everybody needs to reach back down the ladder and give someone else a hand up. That's how we do well and also do good—for ourselves individually and as a country. By repairing the ladder as we climb we create the opportunity for everyone to come up from nothing.

I realized I was a winner before I ever knew how to win, or even what winning looks like for someone who looks like me. And the reality is this: winners who believe they are winners will always strike gold in time. This is the legacy that I now want to pass on to the next generation.

I now know I had a unique attitude toward life in the midst of the enormous challenges in my first decade and beyond. But I don't want my positive mindset to be the outlier among my brothers and sisters staring at the broken ladder of economic mobility. I want this positive, persistent, never-quit, relentless-belief-in-yourself way of thinking to be the rule, to be their pathway to getting up that ladder despite all those rickety, falling-apart rungs. I want it to be clear that my real secret sauce is no secret at all; it is a mental software upgrade accessible to all.

I'll say it again: America is not a country, she is an idea. If we don't like the idea, we can simply reimagine it. That's our mental upgrade.

We can start with reimagining how we see our ourselves: as winners, together. We can get our banks back into the "yes" business so that entrepreneurship can thrive. We can encourage belief in our neighborhoods. We can educate our kids to be producers. We can stake the next generation—all groups, no matter where they came from.

I want the next social movement to be in the suites, not the streets. I want it to be about overcoming class and poverty for all, more so than race (even though race continues to be an issue, of course). I am working on a conscious movement toward reimagining the greatness that America always intended to be: a place—the place—that everyone in the world wants to find their way to so they can secure for themselves that elusive thing we call freedom.

I am asking that every person—the survivors, the thrivers, and the winners—all do their part to live up to America's promise, the promise that where you come from doesn't matter nearly as much as where you're going. Because whatever goes around really does come around.

What I want you to get out of my story is not some kind of magical up-from-nothing tale, but really the story of all of us. My goal every week is to become more and more like the eagle in thoughts and deeds, and less and less like the turkey and the buzzard. Why is all of this self-reflection so very important? Because I cannot love you unless I love me first. I cannot like you, unless I like me first. You cannot expect me to respect you, unless I respect myself first.

And the most powerful statement of them all: if I don't have a real purpose in my life, I am going to make your life a living hell. The most dangerous person in America—and *to* America—is a person with no hope.

At its core, the American Dream means there is always hope if we choose it. We can always choose UP.

NOTES

Chapter 1

1. https://www.charlestonchronicle.net/2018/11/24/there-are-over-2-million-black-owned-businesses-in-the-u-s/.

2. Michael Bloomberg, accessed March 27, 2020, https://www.mikebloomberg.com/news/mike-bloomberg-announces-the-greenwood-initiative.

3. Freedman's Savings Bank, accessed May 18, 2020, http://freedmansbank.org/.

4. https://usafacts.org/articles/federal-farm-subsidies-what-data-says/.

5. Susan K. Urahn et al., "Pursuing the American Dream: Economic Mobility Across Generations," Pew Charitable Trusts, July 2012, https://www.pewtrusts.org/~/media/legacy/uploadedfiles/wwwpewtrustsorg/reports/economic_mobility/pursuingamericandreampdf.pdf.

6. Alina Selyukh, "Will Your Job Still Exist in 2030?," NPR.org, July 11, 2019, https://www.npr.org/2019/07/11/740219271/will-your-job-still-exist-in-2030.

7. Cindy Boren, "The NBA's China-Daryl Morey Backlash, Explained," *Washington Post*, October 7, 2019, https://www.washingtonpost.com/sports/2019/10/07/nba-china-tweet-daryl-morey/.

Chapter 2

1. Lerone Bennett Jr., "Benjamin Elijah Mays: The Last of the Great Schoolmasters," *Ebony,* September 2004, 172.

Chapter 3

1. *The Memo: Five Rules for Your Economic Liberation* (Oakland, CA: Berrett-Koehler, 2017).

2. Akilah Johnson, "That Was No Typo: The Median Net Worth of Black Bostonians Really Is $8," *Boston Globe*, December 11, 2017, https://www.bostonglobe.com/metro/2017/12/11/that-was-typo-the-median-net-worth-black-bostonians-really/ze5kxC1jJelx24M3pugFFN/story.html.

3. Clarence Avant, *The Black Godfather*, documentary, Netflix, directed by Reginald Huldin, released June 7, 2019.

Chapter 4

1. Research completed by Natasha Foreman.

2. Deepak Chopra, *The Seven Laws of Spiritual Success: A Practical Guide to the Fulfillment of Your Dreams* (Strawberry Hills, NSW: Read How You Want, 2008), 61.

Chapter 5

1. Jim Burress, "The Time Coca-Cola Got White Elites in Atlanta to Honor Martin Luther King Jr.," NPR, April 4, 2015, https://www.npr.org/sections/codeswitch/2015/04/04/397391510/when-corporations-take-the-lead-on-social-change.

2. Georgia State University website, accessed March 30, 2020, https://aysps.gsu.edu/andrew-young-biography/.

RESOURCES

If you are a Survivor and want to transition to a Thriver, here are the Operation HOPE, Inc. (HOPE) programs designed to help you grow.

- ► HOPE Inside for Kids: Youth Financial Literacy
- ► HOPE Inside for Adults: Credit and Money Management
- ► HOPE Inside the Workplace: Employee Financial Wellness
- ► HOPE Inside Disaster: Financial Disaster Preparedness & Recovery

If you are a Thriver and want to be a Winner and, eventually, a Philanthropist, here are the HOPE programs that will get you there.

- ► HOPE Inside for Kids: Youth Entrepreneurship | Job Skills
- ► HOPE Inside for Adults: Homeownership
- ► HOPE Inside for Adults: Small Business Development | Entrepreneurial Training Program

If you are a Winner and believe in "Doing Well and Doing Good," please contact me, or the head of HOPE Partners, to learn more about how you can be part of HOPE's Philanthropists, with $.87 of every dollar directly expended on providing free services to Americans seeking to build financial stability and wealth. HOPE would announce your involvement as a HOPE Commitment featured at the HOPE Global Forum.

Please visit operationhope.org to learn more about HOPE's programs.

ACKNOWLEDGMENTS

First and foremost, I would like to thank my wife, Chaitra Dalton Bryant, for being a centered, high frequency, and nourishing safe haven for me. Your support and encouragement, and tips on healthy living, help me keep up with my aggressive schedule and achieve a sense of balance and fulfillment. Thank you so much, love.

Special thanks to my family for their love and support, including my mother, Juanita Smith, Dr. David Dalton, Mrs. Amy "Penny-Mom" Dalton, Mara Hoskins Thomas, Adam Miller, Dave and Annette Harris, Arlene Hayes, and, posthumously, my father, Johnnie Will Smith.

To those who have dedicated their lives to being part of my lifelong mission to eradicate poverty, those who fight with me in the trenches at Operation HOPE, Inc., I say thank you. Namely, Rod McGrew, Rachael Doff, Lance Triggs, Mary Ehrsam, Jena Roscoe, Sirjames Buchanon, Brian Betts, Elaine Hungenberg, Kevin Boucher, Debbie Fiddyment, Tina Fair, Debra Collins, and the entire, past and present, Operation HOPE family. You are my "special forces" unit, and I am proud to work alongside each of you.

To the friends, partners, board members, and supporters of me and the Silver Rights Movement, including (but certainly not limited to) Bill Rogers, Bryan Jordan, Herb Allen III, Tom Brokaw, Phil Griffin, Jeff Schmid, Tim Wennes, Steve Ryan, Jed York, Dr. Cecil "Chip" Murray, Bishop Charles E. Blake, US Comptroller Joseph Otting, Phil Wenger, Ellen Alemany, Ed Bastian, Henry Ford III, Janice Bryant Howroyd, Carlos Vazquez, David Mooney, Calvin Dunning, Mike Hart, Staci Glenn Short, Gina Proia, Sherrice Davis, Toni Dechario, Skip Dillard, Arlen Gelbard, Ed Kramer, Robert Marchman, Kyle Matter, Lissa Miller, Curt Myers, Brian Vittek, Eli Marks, William Cheeks, Kwanza Hall, Allan Kamensky, Susan Somersille Johnson, Lisa Lunday, Sharon Jeffries-Jones, Stephanie Couser, Jon Davies, Robert Harris, William Hanna, Richard Hartnack, Lynn Carter, Tim Chrisman, Roland Martin, Rev. Dr. C. T. Vivian, Dr. Bernice King, Clifford "Tip—T. I." Harris, Tommy Dortch, and Cassius Butts, among many others.

To my publishing and marketing/public relations teams, who work tirelessly to package and promote the message I want to share with the world, including Neal Maillet, Danielle Goodman, Pilar Queen, Bill Mendel, Sarah Trout, Irfan Jafrey, Allison Johnson, and Khallilah Watkins.

Danielle Goodman is simply one of the best editors in the business: her professionalism and work ethic; her positive, get-it-done attitude; and her "this is not just a job" sense of mission from beginning to end. This is the magic sauce of Danielle Goodman. Her passion was evident in my last bestselling book *The Memo* and it became a transformational asset to this book. She listened to and understood, and ultimately learned to channel my voice, when I was not available for an immediate change or edit needed for the manuscript. She was always right on point with what I meant—and what an author truly means is everything to an author. In many ways, Danielle spiritually co-wrote the underlying energy of this book with me, and for that I will be eternally grateful.

Heartfelt thanks to those who took the time to read early drafts of the book, and who provided valuable feedback and statements of support, including Ambassador Andrew Young, Quincy Jones, Roger Goodell, Timothy Welsh, Bishop T. D. Jakes, Brad Hanson, Aron Levine, Susan Taylor, Dallas Tanner, Brad Smith, Susie Buffett, Frank Martell, Lisa Borders, Sarah Friar, Ed Martinez, Dikembe Mutombo, Lindo and Zondwa Mandela, Dan Schulman, John Bartling, and Rahel Getachew, among others.

To my extended family at CNBC Squawk Box, including Andrew Ross Sorkin, Rebecca Quick, Joe Kernan, Jacqueline Corba, and Maxwell Meyers, thank you for welcoming me as a regular guest cohost and for fostering a platform that embraces the sharing of diverse and disruptive perspectives.

To the leadership and the team at the Promise Homes Company, including Tony Ressler, Michael Arougheti, Jackie Williams, Megan McNulty, Michael Chiert, and Demetrius Myatt, thank you for your vision, investment, and dedication to creating a sustainable housing model focused on the advancement and financial uplift of its residents.

And finally, to all of my teachers, mentors, and inspirers who have helped to educate me, formally and informally, to success...up from nothing—thank you for investing in me.

INDEX

ABOUT THE AUTHOR

John Hope Bryant is an American entrepreneur, author, philanthropist, and prominent thought leader on financial inclusion, economic empowerment, and financial dignity. Bryant is the founder, chairman, and chief executive officer of Operation HOPE, Inc.; chairman and chief executive officer of Bryant Group Ventures; and cofounder of Global Dignity. His work has been officially recognized by the last five US presidents, and he has served as an advisor to the last three sitting US presidents. He is responsible for financial literacy becoming the policy of the US federal government. In January 2016, Bryant became the only private American citizen to inspire the renaming of a building on the White House campus when the US Treasury Annex Building was renamed the Freedman's Bank Building. The Freedman's Bank legacy has become the narrative of the work of Operation HOPE—to help all people become fully integrated into our nation's economy.

A member of the founding class of the Forum of Young Global Leaders, and founding member of the Clinton Global Initiative, Bryant is a LinkedIn Influencer, contributor to the *Huffington Post* and *Black Enterprise,* and a member of the World Economic Forum's Expert Network. His Facebook Live "Silver Rights" Series has received millions of views and serves as an engaging platform to foster essential discussion in the digital space around financial inclusion and social uplift. He has received hundreds of awards and citations for his work, including Oprah Winfrey's Use Your Life Award and the John Sherman Award for Excellence in Financial Education from the US Treasury.

In 1994, Bryant was named one of *Time* magazine's 50 Leaders for the Future; two decades later, *American Banker* magazine's 2016 Innovator of the Year. Bryant is the author of three other books: *The Memo: Five Rules for Your Economic Liberation* (Berrett-Koehler), *How the Poor Can Save Capitalism: Rebuilding the Path to the Middle Class* (Berrett-Koehler), and *Love Leadership: The New Way to Lead in a Fear-Based World* (Jossey-Bass).

ABOUT OPERATION HOPE

The mission of Operation HOPE, Inc., is "silver rights" empowerment, making free enterprise work for everyone. We accomplish this through our work on the ground as the nonprofit private banker for the working poor, the under-served, and the struggling middle class. We achieve our mission by being the best-in-class provider of financial literacy empowerment for youth, financial capability for communities, and, ultimately, financial dignity for all.

Since its inception in 1992, HOPE has served more than 2.8 million individuals and has directed more than $3.2 billion in private capital to America's low-wealth communities. It maintains a growing army of twenty-six thousand HOPE Corps volunteers and currently serves more than three hundred US cities—as well as Morocco, Saudi Arabia, South Africa, and the United Arab Emirates. For more, please visit http://www.operationhope.org.

Also by John Hope Bryant

The Memo

Five Rules for Your Economic Liberation

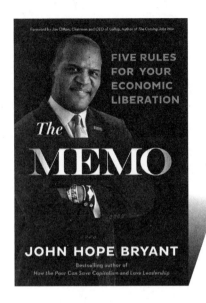

John Hope Bryant, founder and CEO of Operation HOPE, illuminates the path toward liberation that is hiding in plain sight. His message is simple: the supermajority of people who live in poverty, whom Bryant calls the invisible class, as well as millions in the struggling middle class, haven't gotten "the memo"—until now. Building on his personal experience of rising up from economically disadvantaged circumstances and his work with Operation HOPE, Bryant teaches readers five rules that lay the foundation for achieving financial freedom.

Print, hardcover, ISBN 978-1-5230-8456-2
Print, paperback, ISBN 978-1-5230-8866-9
PDF ebook, ISBN 978-1-5230-8457-9
ePub ebook, ISBN 978-1-5230-8458-6
Digital audio, ISBN 978-1-5230-8460-9

Berrett–Koehler Publishers, Inc.
www.bkconnection.com   **800.929.2929**

Also by John Hope Bryant

How the Poor Can Save Capitalism

Rebuilding the Path to the Middle Class

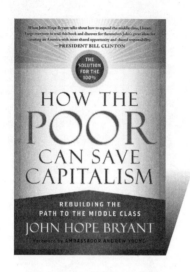

In this visionary book, Operation HOPE founder and successful business-man John Hope Bryant offers a strategy for revitalizing the American dream by investing in the prosperity and education of disadvantaged communities. He exposes the historical roots of poverty, explains why the solutions tried so far have proved insufficient, and lays out what he calls the HOPE Plan, a series of straightforward, actionable steps to build financial literacy and expand opportunity. Consumer spending drives 70 percent of the American economy, but too many people have too much month left at the end of their money. Bryant shows how we can create a thriving economy that works not just for the 1 percent or even the 99 percent but for the 100 percent.

Print, hardcover, ISBN 978-1-62656-032-1
Print, paperback, ISBN 978-1-62656-557-9
PDF ebook, ISBN 978-1-62656-033-8
ePub ebook, ISBN 978-1-62656-034-5

Berrett–Koehler Publishers, Inc.
www.bkconnection.com

800.929.2929

Dear reader,

Thank you for picking up this book and welcome to the worldwide BK community! You're joining a special group of people who have come together to create positive change in their lives, organizations, and communities.

What's BK all about?

Our mission is to connect people and ideas to create a world that works for all.

Why? Our communities, organizations, and lives get bogged down by old paradigms of self-interest, exclusion, hierarchy, and privilege. But we believe that can change. That's why we seek the leading experts on these challenges—and share their actionable ideas with you.

A welcome gift

To help you get started, we'd like to offer you a **free copy** of one of our bestselling ebooks:

www.bkconnection.com/welcome

When you claim your **free ebook**, you'll also be subscribed to our blog.

Our freshest insights

Access the best new tools and ideas for leaders at all levels on our blog at ideas.bkconnection.com.

Sincerely,

Your friends at Berrett-Koehler